BOYCOTTED

AND OTHER STORIES

TALBOT BAINES REED

Boycotted, and other Stories

Talbot Baines Reed

© 1st World Library, 2009
PO Box 2211
Fairfield, IA 52556
www.1stworldlibrary.com
First Edition

LCCN: 2009923501

Softcover ISBN: 978-1-4218-8887-3
Hardcover ISBN: 978-1-4218-8986-3
eBook ISBN: 978-1-4218-8788-3

Purchase *"Boycotted, and other Stories"*
as a traditional bound book at:
www.1stWorldLibrary.com/purchase.asp?ISBN=978-1-4218-8887-3

1st World Library is a literary, educational organization
dedicated to:

- Creating a free internet library of downloadable ebooks

- Hosting writing competitions and offering book publishing
scholarships.

1ˢᵗ World Library Literary Society

Giving Back to the World

"If you want to work on the core problem, it's early school literacy."

- James Barksdale, former CEO of Netscape

"No skill is more crucial to the future of a child, or to a democratic and prosperous society, than literacy."

- Los Angeles Times

"Literacy... means far more than learning how to read and write... The aim is to transmit... knowledge and promote social participation."

- UNESCO

"Literacy is not a luxury, it is a right and a responsibility. If our world is to meet the challenges of the twenty-first century we must harness the energy and creativity of all our citizens."

- President Bill Clinton

"Parents should be encouraged to read to their children, and teachers should be equipped with all available techniques for teaching literacy, so the varying needs and capacities of individual kids can be taken into account."

- Hugh Mackay

CHAPTER ONE

SUB-CHAPTER I

THE SCHOOL CUTS ME

I hardly know yet what it was all about, and at the time I had not an idea. I don't think I was more of a fool than most fellows of my age at Draven's, and I rather hope I wasn't an out-and-out cad.

But when it all happened, I had my doubts on both points, and could explain the affair in no other way than by supposing I must be like the lunatic in the asylum, who, when asked how he came to be there, said, "I said the world was mad, the world said I was mad; the world was bigger than I was, so it shut me up here!"

It had been a dismal enough term, as it was, quite apart from my troubles. That affair of Browne had upset us all, and taken the spirit out of Draven's. We missed him at every turn. What was the good of getting up the football fifteen when our only "place-kick" was gone? Where was the fun in the "Saturday nights" when our only comic singer, our only reciter, our only orator wasn't there? Who cared about giving study suppers or any other sociable entertainment, when there was no Browne to invite?

Browne had left us suddenly. One day he had been the life and soul of Draven's, next morning he had been summoned to Draven's study, and that same evening we saw him drive off to the station in a cab with his portmanteau on the top.

Very few of the fellows knew why he had been expelled. I scarcely knew myself, though I was his greatest chum. On the morning of the day he left, he met me on his way back from Draven's study.

"I'm expelled, Smither," he said, with a dismal face.

"Go on," replied I, taking his arm and scrutinising his face to see where the joke was hidden. But it was no joke.

"I am," said he hopelessly: "I am to go this evening. It's my own fault. I've been a cad. I was led into it. It's bad enough; but I'm not such a blackleg as Draven makes out—"

And here for the first time in my life I saw Browne look like breaking down.

He wasn't going to let me see it, and hurried away before I could find anything to say.

If he hadn't told me himself, I should have called any one who told me Browne had been a cad—well, I'd better not say what I should have called him. I knew my chum had been a rollicking sort of fellow, who found it hard to say No to anybody who asked anything of him; but that he was a blackleg I, for one, would not believe, for all the Dravens in the world.

Hardly knowing what I did, I walked up to the master's study door and knocked.

"Come in." I could tell by the voice that came through the door I should do no good.

I went in. Mr Draven was pacing up and down the room, and stopped short in front of me as I entered. "Well?"

I wished I was on the other side of the door; but I wasn't, and must say something, however desperate.

"Please, sir, Browne—"

"Browne leaves here to-day," said Mr Draven coldly; "what do you want?"

"Please, sir, I hope you will—"

I forgot where I was and what I was saying. My mind wandered aimlessly, and I ended my sentence I don't know how.

Draven saw I was confused, and wasn't unkind.

"You have been a friend of Browne, I know," he said, "and you are sorry. So am I, terribly sorry," and his voice quite quavered as he spoke.

There was a pause, and I made a frantic effort to recall my scattered thoughts.

"Won't you let him off this time, sir?" I gasped.

"That, Smither, is out of the question," said the head master, so steadily and incisively that I gave it up, and left the room without another word. The fellows were trooping down the passage to breakfast, little guessing the secret of my miserable looks, or the reason why Browne was not in his usual place.

But the secret came out, and the school staggered under the shock. Mr Draven announced our comrade's departure kindly enough in the afternoon, adding that he had confessed the offence for which he was expelled, and was penitent. Two hours later we saw his cab drive off, and as we watched it disappear it all seemed to us like a hideous dream.

We said little about it to one another. We did not even care to inquire particularly into the offence for which he had suffered. But we moped and missed him at every turn, and wished the miserable term were ending instead of beginning.

This, however, is a long digression. I sat down to write the story of my own trouble, not Browne's. But the reader will understand now why I said that, as it was, apart from my own misfortunes, the term, which had still a month more to run when my story begins, had been a dismal one.

* * * * *

I was wandering about the playground one frosty November morning, beginning to hope that if a frost should come we might after all get a little fun at Draven's before the holidays came, when Odger junior, whistling shrilly, crossed my path.

Odger junior was not exactly my fag, for we had no fags at Draven's, and if we had had, I had not yet reached that pitch of dignity at which one fellow has the right to demand the services of another. Still Odger junior had, for a consideration, done a good many odd jobs for me, and I had got into the way of regarding him as a quasi-fag.

"Hullo, youngster!" said I, as we met, "there's going to be a

Talbot Baines Reed

stunning frost. Can't you smell it in the air? I wish you'd cut down to Bangle's and get me a pair of straps for my skates."

To my astonishment, not wholly unmixed with amusement, Odger junior regarded me majestically for a moment, and then, ejaculating the oracular phrase, "Oh, ah!" walked off, his four-foot-one drawn to its full height, his hands behind his back, and his mouth still drawn up for whistling, but apparently too overcome with dignity to emit the music which an observer would naturally be led to expect.

I was not on the whole a short-tempered youth. My laziness saved me from that. It certainly did occur to me on this bright frosty morning that it would be exhilarating both for young Odger and me if I were to go after him and kick him. But what was the use? He would enjoy it as much as I should. There would be plenty of ways in which to pay him out less fatiguing than an undignified chase round the playground. So I let him go, and grinned to think how much nicer monkeys are when they behave like monkeys, and not like men.

I had a lot of work to do in my study that morning before afternoon school, and so had very little time to think of Odger junior, or any one else. As it was, I was only just in time to take my usual place in the Greek class when Mr Draven sailed into the room and the lesson began.

I had been so flurried by my hasty arrival that I did not at first observe that the desk on my right, usually occupied by a boy called Potter, was vacant.

"Where's Potter?" I asked of my neighbour on the left. "Is he—why, there he is at Browne's old desk!" I added, catching sight of the deserter across the room.

Browne's desk had always been left empty since its late owner went. None of us had cared to appropriate it, and the sight of it day after day had fed our sorrow over his loss. It seemed to me, therefore, an act almost of disloyalty on Potter's part towards the memory of my old chum to install himself coolly at his desk without saying a word to anybody.

"What's he gone there for?" I inquired of Sadgrove on my left. "He's got no—"

"Don't talk to me!" said Sadgrove.

Sadgrove was in a temper, and I wasn't surprised. So was I, lazy as I was. We had all stuck to Browne through the term, and it was a little too much now to find a fellow like Potter, who professed to be Browne's friend too, stepping in this cold-blooded way into his place. Sadgrove was put up to construe, so there was no opportunity for further conversation, had we desired it.

I wasn't surprised that Potter avoided me in the playground after school. He guessed, I supposed, what I had to say to him, and had the decency to be ashamed of himself. However, I was determined to have it out, and that evening, after preparation, went up to his study. He was there, and looked guilty enough when he saw me.

"Look here, Potter," I began, trying to be friendly in spite of all. I got no further, for Potter, without a word, walked out of the door, leaving me standing alone in the middle of his study.

I had seen the working of a guilty conscience once or twice before at Draven's, but never knew it to work in quite so strange a manner as it did with Potter that evening.

There was nothing for it but to give him up as a bad job, and go to bed. Which I did; and awoke next morning in a forgiving mood.

It was always a scramble at breakfast on Saturdays at Draven's to see who could get nearest to the ham, for we sickened of the cold mutton they gave us on other days. This morning, to my gratification, I was "well up." That is, there were only two fellows before me, so that at any rate I was good for a fair, straight slice from the middle.

"Huzza!" said I, crowding up to Williams, who was next above me. "I've never had anything but knuckle all this—"

Williams faced round as he heard my voice; and then, without waiting to hear the end of my sentence, got up and took a seat at the lower end of the table.

"Poor beggar's out of sorts," said I to myself. "Another of his bilious attacks, I suppose," I added, moving up to his seat and addressing the proud occupant of the carver's chair. This fellow was Harrison, whom, next to Browne, we counted the oiliest fellow at Draven's. He could sing, and make puns, and though a long way behind Browne, was a popular, jovial companion.

He appeared not to hear my remark, but, hitching his chair a little away, began deliberately to carve a slice of ham.

He took a long time about it, and I watched him patiently till he was done. It was a prime ham, I could see, and, ashamed as I am to confess it, it made me feel amiable to all the world to find it was so.

"If they were all like this—" I began.

"There's room here, Harrison, old man," Williams called up the table.

Whereupon Harrison, plate in hand, went down to keep Williams company, leaving me for the first time in my life "top-hammer."

Somehow I did not enjoy the dignity quite as much as I should have expected. I was sorry Harrison had gone, for I wanted to speak to him about Potter, and I could not help fancying, from his unusual manner, that he was put out about something, and I thought he might have told me about it instead of chumming up to Williams. However, I was hungry, and took my slice of ham and passed the dish along to the fellow next me, who sat below the two empty chairs up which I had risen.

It was rather a solitary meal, and I was glad when it was over and the bell rang for first school. There at least I should have the society of the sympathetic Sadgrove, who, as I knew, felt as sore as I did about Potters behaviour.

But, to my mortification as well as perplexity, Sadgrove I found, had cleared out his desk and removed his goods and chattels to a seat on the row behind mine, where he appeared to have met with a cordial welcome from his new neighbours.

I could not make it out. He always told me he liked his desk better than any, and would not change it even for Browne's. And here he was, for no apparent reason, on a lower form, at a smaller desk, and in—well, less select society.

As I sat in my place that morning, with an empty desk on each side of me, it began slowly to dawn on my mind that something was wrong somewhere.

Talbot Baines Reed

The proceedings of Odger junior, Potter, Sadgrove, Williams, and Harrison, taken singly, were not of much importance, but taken as a whole I did not like them. I might be wrong. There might be no intention to cut me, and I could not think of anything I had done or said which would account for it. I would try, at any rate, to get to the bottom of it before I was many hours older.

So I went in search of my cousin, who was a few months my senior, and a particular chum of Williams.

"I say, Arthur, what did Williams cut me dead for this morning?"

Arthur looked uncomfortable and said—

"How should I know?"

"You do know," said I, "and I want to know why."

He coloured up, and made as though he would leave room. But my blood was up, and I stepped across door.

"Tell me this," I said. "Have these fellows cut on purpose or no?"

"However should—"

"You do know. Are they cutting me or no?"

He flushed up again, and then said hurriedly—

"Yes, we are!"

SUB-CHAPTER II

I AM BEATEN

"Yes, we are."

The reader may think it strange when I tell him that my first sensation on receiving this momentous announcement was one of almost amusement, I knew it was a mistake, and that I had done nothing to merit the sentence which had been passed upon me. Draven's had put itself in the wrong, and I had pride enough to determine that I of all people was not going out of my way to put it right.

So I took my cousin's announcement coolly, and refrained from demanding any further explanations.

"Oh!" I said, with something like a sneer, and walked off; leaving him, so I flattered myself, rather snubbed.

I was boycotted!

There was something a trifle flattering in the situation. Brave men before my time had been boycotted. I had read their stories, and sympathised with them, and hated (as I hate still) the miscreants who, in the name of "patriotism" had acted the sneak's and coward's part to ruin them. Now I was going to taste something of their hardships at the hands of my "patriotic" schoolfellows; and my spirit rose as I resolved to hold up my head with the bravest of them.

Forewarned is forearmed; and when I went into school that afternoon I gave no one a chance of avoiding me. I spread myself out as comfortably as possible at my place, and shifted some of the papers and books which crowded my

Talbot Baines Reed

own desk into the vacant desks on either side of me, first ejecting rather ostentatiously a few papers and notebooks which had been left in them by their late owners.

I was conscious of one or two glances directed my way across the room; but these only added to my pleasure as I emptied Sadgrove's inkpot into my own, and proceeded cheerfully to cut my initials on Williams's desk. When I was put up to construe, I managed to get through my passage without any sign of trepidation; and when at last the class was dismissed, I took the wind out of the sails of my boycotters by remaining some minutes later than any one else, completing the decoration of my new quarters.

It was easy enough in the playground that afternoon to keep clear of my fellow human beings; and I had, as I persuaded myself, a jolly hour in the gymnasium all by myself. Fellows looked in at the door now and then, but did not disturb my peace; and it was rather gratifying than otherwise to feel that as long as I chose to occupy the place every one else would have to wait outside.

"After all," thought I, as I went to bed that night, "boycotting isn't as bad as people make it out. I've had all I wanted to-day. No one has annoyed me or injured me. I can do pretty much as I like; in fact, I do more than I ever used to be able to do. If any one is loser by it all, it's the other fellows, and not me. I rather enjoy it."

"Still," I could not help reflecting; as I turned over and went to sleep, "I think Harrison might have stuck by me."

When I woke next morning it was with a sense of something on my mind. I tried hard to persuade myself it was amusement, and went down to breakfast wondering how Draven's would keep it up. I found myself "top- hammer" again—or I should say "top-muttoner," for ham was a luxury reserved only for one day in the week—and the two chairs below me were again vacant.

I helped myself to a slice from the uninviting joint, and then artlessly pushed the dish along one place, opposite the first of the empty chairs, and proceeded to regale myself.

It was interesting to see the perplexity which my simple manoeuvre caused. The next fellow below me, out of reach three chairs away, had nothing for it but either to speak to me, which I calculated his vows would not allow him to do, or else ignominiously to walk up to the seat next mine and possess himself of the dish. He did the latter, and I scored one—the only "one" I scored for some time to come.

For Draven's, seeing I was defiant, felt hurt in its pride, and drew the blockade closer around me. It had expected at least that I should make some effort to win my way back into popularity, and it did not at all like, when it chose to boycott me, that I should boycott it. So gradually we forgot what the quarrel was about, and set ourselves to see who could hold out longest.

A manly, sensible, Christian occupation for fifty fellow-creatures during a dull winter month!

I never got the gymnasium to myself now, for whenever I went it was always full, and remained full till I was tired of waiting for a vacant bar or swing. As for football, hockey, paper-chasing, and the other school sports, I was, of course, excluded both by my own pride and the action of the school.

In fact, Draven's never pulled together so well at anything as they did at boycotting me during those few weeks. Their discipline was splendid. They all seemed to know exactly

Talbot Baines Reed

what to do and what not to do when I appeared on the scene, and any hopes I had of winning over a few stragglers to my side vanished before the blockade had lasted a week.

At first I didn't mind it. My mettle was up, I was excited, and the consciousness that I was unjustly treated carried me through.

But in a few days the novelty began to wear off, and I began to get tired of my own company. I still made the most of my elbow-room in class and at meals, but it ceased to be amusing.

I tried to work hard in my study every evening, and to persuade myself I was glad of the opportunity of making up for lost time; but somehow or other the distant sounds of revelry and laughter made Livy and Euclid more dull and uninteresting than ever. I tried to hug myself with the notion of how independent I was in school and out, how free I was from bores, how jolly the long afternoon walks were with no one hanging on at my heels, how dignified it was to hold up my head when all the world was against me. But spite of it all I moped.

Greatly to my disgust, Draven's did not mope. As I sat down in my study, or wandered, still more solitary, in the crowded playground, it seemed as if all the school except myself had never been in better spirits. Fellows seemed to have shaken off the cloud which Browne's expulsion had left behind. The football team was better than it had been for a year or two, and I overheard fellows saying that the "Saturday nights" were jollier even than last winter. In fact, it seemed as if, like Jonah, the throwing of me overboard had brought fine weather all round.

Still I was not going to give in. Draven's should be ashamed of itself before I met it half way!

So I watched with satisfaction my face growing pale day by day, and I aided this new departure in my favour by eating less than usual, giving up outdoor exercise, and staying up late over my lessons.

I calculated that at the rate I was going I should be reduced to skin and bones by the end of my term, and perhaps at my funeral Draven's would own they had wronged me. At present, however, my pallor seemed to escape their observation, and as for my late hours, all the good they did me was an imposition from Mr Draven for breaking rules.

As the days went on, I seemed to have dropped altogether out of life. I might have been invisible, for anything any one seemed to see of me. Even the masters appeared to have joined in the conspiracy to ignore me, and for a whole week I sat at my solitary desk without hearing the sound of my own voice.

My readers may scoff when I tell them that at the end of a fortnight I felt like running away. The silence and isolation which had amused me at first became a slow torture at last, and, poor-spirited wretch that I was, my only comfort was in now and then crying in bed in the dark.

I made up for this secret weakness by putting on a swagger in public, and rendered myself ridiculous in consequence. Draven's could hardly help being amused by a fellow who one day slunk in and out among them self-consciously pale, black under the eyes, with a hacking cough and a funereal countenance, and the next blustered about defiantly and glared at every one he met.

The fact was, having despaired of making a friend, my one

Talbot Baines Reed

longing now was to make an enemy. I would have paid all my pocket-money twice over for a quarrel or a fight with somebody. But that was a luxury harder to get even than a friendly word.

I tried one day.

I was mooning disconsolately round the playground, when I met young Wigram, the most artless youngster in all Draven's.

"You played up well in the second fifteen on Saturday," I said, as if I had spoken to him not five minutes ago, whereas, as a matter of fact, the sound of my own voice gave me quite a shock.

"Yes," began he, falling into the snare, "I was lucky with that run up from—er—I—beg pardon—good-bye," and he bolted precipitately.

It was a mild victory as far as it went, but it did not end there, for that afternoon I came upon a group in the playground, the central figure of which was the wretched Wigram, on his knees in the act of apologising humbly all round for having been cad enough to speak to me. It seemed a good chance for the long-wished-for quarrel, and I jumped at it.

"Let him go!" shouted I, breaking into the group and addressing the company generally. "If any one touches him he will have to fight me!"

Alas! they stared a little, and then laughed a little, and then strolled away, with Wigram among them, leaving me alone. After that I knew I was beaten, and might as well own it, for a disappointed enemy is a far worse failure than a disappointed friend.

Still I clung on to my pride. Broken down as I was, and unnerved and damaged in my self-respect, there was but a week more of the term to run, and I would try to hold out till the end. If I could only do that, I was safe, for I would get my father to take me away at Christmas for good. No— would I?—that would be the biggest surrender of all. I could not think what I would do.

So I sat down and wrote to Browne for lack of any better occupation, and told him how I envied him his expulsion, and wished any such luck could happen to me.

Then I grimly set myself to endure the remaining days of my slow torture.

Oh, the silence of those days! The noise and laughter of the fellows was nothing to it. I could endure the one, and in my extremity was even glad of it. But the sealed lips of everyone that met me were like so many daggers.

At last I was really ill—or at any rate I was so reduced that unless relief came soon I must either capitulate or run away.

Even yet I found it hard to contemplate the former alternative. I met Harrison one morning in the passage. I suppose I must have looked specially miserable, for, contrary to his usual practice now, instead of looking away, he slackened speed as he came up and looked at me. Now was my time surely. I was famished for want of a friendly word or look, and my pride was at its last gasp. I believe I had actually begun to speak, when a sound in the passage startled us both, and we passed by as of old—strangers.

I rushed off to my study, ashamed and disappointed, and paced round it like a caged animal. What could I do? Should I write to some of the fellows? Should I tell Draven? or—

Talbot Baines Reed

should I escape?

Then it occurred to me, had not I a right to know why I was being treated like this? What had I done? Was I a sneak, or a leper, or a murderer, that I should thus be excommunicated and tortured? What a fool I had been, not to think of this before! Alas! it was too late now. My pride had made it impossible for me to speak the first word without surrendering all along the line; and even yet, at the eleventh hour, I could not face that. So I shut myself up for another day, miserable, nervous, and ill, and counted the minutes to bedtime.

The evening post brought a letter from Browne, and, thankful for any diversion, and the silent company even of a friendly piece of paper, I crawled off early to my study to make the most of my little comfort.

I started before I had read two lines, and uttered an exclamation of amazement.

"Dear Smither,—

"There's been a most frightful mistake. By the same post as brought your letter I got enclosed from Williams. What a set of cads they've been, and all my fault! I've written to Williams that if it's not all put right in twenty-four hours I'll come down, disgraced as I am, and tell Draven. I'm in too great a rage to write more. Unless I get a telegram 'All right!' by ten to-morrow morning I'll come.

"Yours ever,—

"P. Browne."

Williams's letter enclosed—or rather part of it, for Browne

had kept one sheet—was as follows, though my head was swimming so much at the time that I could scarcely take it all in.

"The fellows here haven't forgotten you, and they're showing it in a pretty decided way at present. About three weeks ago we discovered that Smither, who called himself your friend, was the sneak who went to Draven the morning you were expelled, and let out about you. He was seen coming from D.'s study early, and young Wright, who happened to be in the next room, heard him speaking about you. Well, we've boycotted him. Not a fellow is allowed to speak to him, or notice him, or go near him. Everybody's been bound over, and unless some one plays traitor, the place will get too hot for him before the term's up. And serve him right too. Harrison and I—"

Here the letter broke off.

I felt stunned; and, strange to say, the sudden discovery left me as miserable as it found me. I suppose I was ill; but for a short time my passion got the upper hand, and made it worse for me than if I had never known the truth.

But it didn't last long. There came a knock at the door, and, without waiting for an invitation, Harrison came into the room, looking so miserable and scared that I scarcely recognised him for a moment. He was evidently prepared for any sort of rebuff, and I despised myself far more than him as I heard the half-frightened voice in which he began.

"Smither, old man—"

He got no farther; or at least I did not hear any more. It seemed like a dream after that. I was dimly conscious of his hand on my arm and then round me. The next thing I was aware of was that I was lying in bed, with him sitting beside me sponging my forehead.

"Has the bed-bell rung?" I asked.

"My dear fellow, you've been in bed a fortnight," said he, bending over me; "but you mustn't talk now."

After awhile I asked again—

"Why are you here, then?" for the term had had only three days to run when I had been taken ill.

"We couldn't go, old man. The fellows begged Draven to let them stay till you were out of danger, and he did. They're all here. This is Christmas Day, and they will be glad to hear you are better. But really you mustn't talk, please."

"Tell the fellows to go home, then," I said, "and wish them a Merry Christmas, and say—"

"Really, old man," pleaded Harrison, looking quite frightened, "don't talk."

That was the quietest, but not the least hopeful Christmas Day I ever spent.

And when Draven's met again next term, I fancy most of us had got by heart the good Christmas motto, "Goodwill to men," and were mutually agreed that, whatever manly and noble sports we should engage in during the year, boycotting should not be one of them.

CHAPTER TWO

A TRUE STORY IN TWO

SUB-CHAPTER I

THE STORY

Ferriby had broken up. The rats and mice were having their innings in the schoolrooms, and the big bell was getting rusty for want of exercise. The door of the Lower Third had not had a panel kicked out of it for a whole week, and Dr Allsuch's pictures and sofas and piano were all stacked up in the Detention Room while their proper quarters underwent a "doing-up."

There was no mistake about the school having broken up. And yet, if it was so, how came we all to be there this Christmas week, instead of sitting at our own firesides in the bosoms of our own families, anywhere but at Ferriby?

When I say all, I mean all in Jolliffe's House; the others had cleared out. Bull's was empty, and Wragg's, across the quadrangle, had not a ghost of a fellow left. Nor had the doctor's. Every other house was shut up, but Jolliffe's was as full up as the night before a county match, and no sign of an exodus.

Of course the reader guesses the reason at once!

"I know," says one virtuous youth; "they'd all been detained for bad conduct, and stopped their holidays!"

Wrong, my exemplary one! Jolliffe's was the best behaved house in Ferriby, though I say so who should not. But any one could tell you so. For every thousand lines of imposition the other houses had to turn out Jolliffe's only had a hundred, and for every half-dozen canes worn out on the horny palms of Bull's and Wragg's, one was quite enough for us.

No; the fact was, one of our fellows had had scarlet fever a fortnight before the holidays, and as he was in and out with us for some days before it was discovered, sleeping in our dormitory, and sitting next to us in class it was a settled thing we were all in for it.

So the school was suddenly broken up, the other houses all packed off, the sickly ones among us—there were only one or two—removed to the infirmary, and the rest of us, under the charge of Jolliffe himself, invited to make the best of a bad job, and enjoy ourselves as well as we could, with the promise that if in three weeks no one else showed signs of knocking up, we should be allowed to go home.

Of course, we were awfully sold at first, and by no means in an amiable frame of mind. It is no joke to be done out of Christmas at home. What a dolt that Gilks was to get scarlet fever! Why could he not have waited till he got home?

But after a day or two we shook down, as British boys will, to our lot. After all, it was only a case of putting off our holiday, and meanwhile we were allowed to do anything we liked, short of setting the place on fire, or kicking up a row near the infirmary.

There were enough of us to turn out two good teams at football, or to run a big paper-chase across country, or get up a grand concert of an evening; and not too many of us to crowd into the long dormitory, where, for all we were interfered with, we might have prolonged our bolster matches "from eve to dewy morn."

In time we came to look upon our confinement as rather a spree than otherwise, and this feeling was considerably heightened by the arrival of several hampers at the beginning of Christmas week, including a magnificent one from Dr Allsuch himself, along with a message bidding us be sure and have a merry Christmas. We voted the doctor a brick, and drank his health in ginger beer, with great enthusiasm, to the toast of "Dr Allsuch, and all such bricks!"

It was on Christmas Eve, after a specially grand banquet off the contents of one of these hampers, that we crowded round the big common- hall fire in a very complacent frame of mind, uncommonly well satisfied and comfortable within and without.

"I don't know," said Lamb meditatively, cracking a walnut between his finger and thumb, and slowly skinning it—"I don't know; Gilks might have done us a worse turn after all."

"I rather wish he'd make a yearly thing of it," said Ellis. "They say he's pulled through all right."

"Oh yes, he's all right! and so are the other three. In fact, French and Addley never had scarlet fever at all. It was a false alarm."

"Well," said Lamb, "I'm jolly glad of it! I wouldn't have cared for any of them to die, you know."

Lamb said this in a tone as if we should all be rather surprised to hear him say so.

"Nobody ever did die at Ferriby, did they?" said Jim Sparrow, the youngest and tenderest specimen we had at Jolliffe's.

It was rather cheek of a kid like Jim to interpose at all in a conversation of his seniors, and it seemed as if he was going to get snubbed by receiving no reply, when Fergus suddenly took the thing up.

"Eh, young Jim Sparrow, what's that you're saying?"

Fergus was the wag of our house—indeed, he was the only Irishman we could boast of, and the fact of his being an Irishman always made us inclined to laugh whenever he spoke. We could see now by the twinkle in his eye that he was going to let off the steam at Jim Sparrow's expense.

"I said," replied Jim, blushing rather to find every body listening to him, "nobody's ever died at Ferriby, have they?"

Fergus gazed at him in astonishment.

"What!" exclaimed he, "you mean to say you never heard of poor Bubbles?"

"Bubbles? No," replied Jim, looking rather scared.

"Just fancy that!" said Fergus, turning round to us; "never heard of Bubbles!"

Of course we, who saw what the wag was driving at, looked rather surprised and a little mysterious.

"What was it?" inquired Jim Sparrow, looking half ashamed of himself.

"Eh? Well, if you never heard it, I'd better not tell you. It's not a nice story, is it, you fellows?"

"Horrible!" said Lamb, starting at another walnut.

"Oh, do tell me!" cried Jim eagerly, "I'm so fond of stories;" and he settled himself back in his chair rather uneasily, and tried to look as if it was all good fun.

"Well, if you do want it I'll tell you; but don't blame me if it upsets you, that's all!" replied the irrepressible Fergus.

Jim looked as heroic as he could, and wished he had never asked to be enlightened on the subject of Bubbles.

Fergus refreshed himself with an orange, stuck his feet into the fender, and began in a solemn voice.

"I suppose, Jim Sparrow, if you have never heard about Bubbles, you really don't know the history of the school at all. You don't even know how it came to be called Ferriby?"

"No," responded Jim, keeping his eyes on the fire.

"Ferriby is derived from two Anglo-Saxon words," proceeded Fergus, "which you may have heard—'fire' and 'boy.' Now I'll tell you about Bubbles!"

There was something very mysterious about the manner in which Fergus uttered these words, and we listened for what was to come almost as breathlessly as Jim Sparrow.

"It was early in this century," he said, "that a boy came to this school called Bubbles. No one knew where he came from. He had no parents, and never went home for the holidays. He was about your age, Sparrow, and just your build, and he was in the Lower Fourth."

"I'm going to be moved up this Christmas," interposed Jim hurriedly.

"Are you? So was Bubbles going to be moved up when what I'm going to tell you happened!"

It was getting dark, and for the last, few minutes all the light in the room had been caused by a jet of gas in the coals. That jet now went out suddenly, leaving us in nearly total darkness.

"It was a Christmas Eve. Everybody else had gone home for the holidays, and Bubbles was the only boy left in the school—Bubbles and a master whose name I won't mention."

"He was the Detention Master, wasn't he?" inquired Lamb's voice.

"Ah, yes. There's no harm in telling you that. Bubbles and the Detention Master were left all alone at Ferriby, Sparrow."

"Ye—es," said Sparrow softly, and making two syllables of the word.

"They'd had no hampers sent them, and as they sat round the fire that evening they knew both of them there was no Christmas dinner in the house. They had neither of them tasted food for some days, and had no money to buy any, and if they had had, the snow was too deep to get anywhere. They had tried making soup out of copybook covers, but it wasn't nourishing, and the soles of their boots which they tried to eat didn't sit well on their stomachs."

Some one choked at this point, greatly to the speaker's wrath.

"All right; some one seems to think it a laughing matter, so I'll stop."

"Oh no," cried one or two voices eagerly, "do go on. He only got a piece of apple the wrong way."

"Was it you laughed, Jim Sparrow?" demanded Fergus.

"Oh no," replied Jim, who was holding on rather tight to the sides of his chair.

"I don't like any one making fun of a serious thing like this," said Fergus. "I was saying the soles of their boots didn't sit well on their stomachs. They sat round the fire the whole evening, brooding and ravenous, and saying nothing. For a long time they both stared into the fire; then presently the master took his eyes off the fire and stared at Bubbles. Bubbles used to be fat, like you, Sparrow, but the last day or two he had got rather reduced. Still he was fairly plump; at least, so thought the master, as he looked first at him, then at the fire, and then thought of the empty larder downstairs."

It was too dark to see Jim Sparrow, but I could almost *hear* him turn pale, so profound was the silence.

"The fire was a big one, a roaring one, and howled up the chimney as if it was hungry too. Bubbles where he sat was close to it, in fact, his feet almost touched the bars. The master sat a little behind Bubbles, and his arm rested on the

Talbot Baines Reed

back of Bubbles's chair. 'To-morrow,' thought the master, 'he will be thinner, and next day only skin and bone.' Then he thought of the saying in the copy-books, 'Never put off till to- morrow what you can do to-day.' He sprang to his feet, seized Bubbles by the head and feet—there was a shriek and a yell—and next moment the master was alone in the room, and the chimney was on fire!"

At this last sentence the speaker, suiting the action to the word, had risen from his seat and suddenly pounced upon the unhappy Sparrow, who, already paralysed with terror, now fairly yelled and howled for mercy. Fergus dropped him back gently into his chair, and resuming his own seat, continued—

"There is very little to add. Under the ruins were found the remains of the master grasping in each hand a large-sized drumstick. Bubbles was never seen more. It was supposed he escaped without his legs on to the roof, and they do say that every Christmas Eve he revisits Ferriby, and tries to get down the chimney in search of his lost legs."

At the conclusion of this tragic story every one drew a long breath. Jim Sparrow, it was clear, had swallowed it from beginning to end, and one or two others of the juniors looked as if they would have been more pleased had the event not been made to happen on Christmas Eve, of all nights. But with these exceptions the whole thing seemed a very good joke, and greatly to the credit of Fergus's imagination.

"Oh, and I should say," added that doughty historian, as he poked up the fire into a blaze, "though it's not of much consequence, that this took place in this very house, they say in this very room. Funny story, isn't it, Sparrow?"

Sparrow had not yet sufficiently recovered from his fright to reply, but it was evident by his looks he considered it anything but funny. However, the talk soon veered round to other and more ordinary topics, in the midst of which, aided by the remnants of our feast, the spirits even of Jim Sparrow revived, so much so that by bedtime he was as cheerful as if he had never even heard the name of Bubbles.

Talbot Baines Reed

SUB-CHAPTER II

THE GHOST

Mr Jolliffe appeared on the scene as usual at ten o'clock, and read prayers. After which, advising us all to get a good night, and announcing that to-morrow being Christmas Day, we should not breakfast till nine, he trotted off to his quarters and left us.

We were all pretty ready to take his advice, for what with a sixteen- mile run across country in the afternoon, and our big dinner in the evening, the thought of bed seemed rather a comfortable prospect.

One or two of the fellows, however, fellows whom no exertion ever seemed to weary, protested against going to bed at ten o'clock, and took good care that those who did shouldn't sleep. We were used to that, and had to put up with it, and it must have been close upon the stroke of Christmas Day before they finally condescended to turn in and leave us in peace.

One by one the candles went out, the talk and the laughter gradually subsided, and even the grunts and twitches of the doughty heroes as they first gave themselves over to slumber died away in the darkness. For the first time since we rose that morning, a dead silence reigned in Jolliffe's.

In fact, as I lay awake and tried to get to sleep the silence seemed unnaturally profound. The tick of the big clock down in the hall struck on the ear with almost a thud, and the light breeze outside moaned among the ventilators and played chromatic scales through the keyhole in a fashion quite disturbing. I wished that wind would shut up, and that the clock would run down. How was a fellow to get to sleep with such a row going on?

And yet, next moment, the utter silence of the place disturbed me even more than the wind and the clock. Why, I actually seemed to hear the winking of my own eyes as I lay there. I wished some one would snore, or breathe hard, or roll over in his bed. But no, in all those thirty beds there was neither sound nor motion.

Nothing is so unpleasant as listening for sounds in a dead silence. I half wished—

Hullo! what was that? Rain on the window! Why can't rain drop straight instead of tapping at a fellow's window? It sounded like some one wanting to come in. I knew it was only rain; but supposing it *had* been somebody—a thief, for instance, or—or—Bubbles come to look after his legs!

I do not know what evil genius put the thought of Bubbles into my head. But once in, I could not get it out. Downstairs before the big fire I had laughed as loud as any one, and been as sure as sure could be that Fergus's story was all an invention of his fertile imagination. But, somehow, now that the lights were out, and the fellows all asleep, and the wind was moaning outside, and I lay sleepless on my bed, it did not seem so utterly preposterous.

Not that I believed in ghosts. Oh dear no. I hoped I was not such a fool as that, but supposing—

That rain again at the window! Why couldn't it stop startling a fellow in that way? Yes, supposing Fergus's story had been founded on fact, what a dreadful end to a boy Bubbles's end must have been!

"And they do say,"—the words seemed to echo in my ears—"that every Christmas Eve he re-visits Ferriby, and tries to get down the chimney in search of his lost legs."

Ugh! Why did not some of the fellows wake up? How unnaturally still they all were! I would have given all my pocket-money to two of them to start another steeplechase that moment over the beds. In fact, I had half a mind to—

As I reached this point a sudden noise made my blood run cold, and froze me to my bed.

It did not seem to be in the dormitory, or on the stairs outside, or in the quadrangle below. None of my companions appeared to have heard it, for they all slept on quietly, and the silence which followed was doubly as intense as that which had gone before. What could it be?

I do not fancy I was a particularly cowardly boy, but somehow that sound terrified me. I could neither move nor call out. All I could do was to lie and listen.

There it was again! this time not so sudden, but far more distinct. There was no mistaking it now. As sure as I lay there, it was something on the roof! It sounded like something crawling slowly and by fits and starts along the gutter just above the dormitory. Sometimes it seemed to spring upwards, as though attempting to reach a higher position, and then sullenly slip down and proceed on its crawling way.

Yes, without doubt Fergus had told the truth!

Suddenly a voice in a loud whisper at the other end of the dormitory exclaimed—

"Listen! I say, listen!"

It was Lamb's voice. There was at least some comfort in knowing that I was not the only one awake.

With a desperate effort I sat up in my bed and replied—

"Oh, Lamb, what is it?"

His only reply was a gasp, as the noises recommenced. The body, whatever it was, seemed to have dragged itself forward, so as to be now just over our heads. The ceiling above us went right up into the roof, and I could distinctly hear a rustling sound against the tiles, followed by an occasional upward leap, sometimes almost wild in its eagerness. How could I mistake these sounds? The chimney was immediately above us, and it was towards this goal, as I well knew, that the hapless and legless Bubbles was destined fruitlessly to aspire. At last one bound more frantic than the rest, followed by a sudden clatter of displaced tiles, unloosed my tongue, and I fairly cried out—

"Oh!"

Half a dozen fellows were on the alert in an instant.

"Who's that called out?" cried one. "I'd like to scrag him."

"What's the row, whoever it is?" demanded Fergus.

"Hush! Listen!" was all I could reply.

There must have been something in my voice which bespoke my horror, for a dead silence ensued.

But not for long. Once more the dull, dragging sound,

interrupted by the spasmodic and fruitless leaps!

A shudder went round the dormitory at the sound. They knew as well as I did what it meant.

"It's the ghost!" faltered Sparrow's trembling voice; and no one contradicted him. Fergus himself, like one suddenly confronted with a spirit of his own raising, seemed the most terrified of the lot, and I could hear him gasping as he sat petrified in his bed.

"Can't some one strike a light?" Lamb said presently.

All very well, but the matches were on the table, and to secure them one would have to get out of bed. No one seemed quite inclined for that.

As we lay endeavouring to screw up our courage to the necessary pitch, the sound once more recommenced, with a violent motion towards the edge of the roof. The moon at the same moment broke out from behind the clouds and shot its pale light in at the big windows. There was a momentary pause above us, and then, casting a sudden shadow across the dormitory floor, a dim white figure, as of a body without limbs, floated down outside the window. The moon once more was obscured, and we were left motionless and horrified in utter silence and darkness! What would come next?

How long we might have remained in suspense I can't say, had not Lamb and another fellow, by a combined effort of heroism, dashed arm in arm from bed and secured the matches. They were in the act of striking a light (one match had broken, and another had had no head)—they were in the act of striking a light when Lamb, who was close to the window, suddenly exclaimed—"Look!"

There was such terror in his tone that we knew only too well what he had seen. But where!

"Where?" I managed to gasp.

"There, down in the quad," he replied, pointing out of the window, but looking another way.

Curiosity is sometimes greater than fear, and for all my terror I could not resist the impulse to steal up to the window and look out. And others did the same.

It was as Lamb had said. There in the quadrangle below, moving restlessly to and fro, and swaying itself upward, as if in supplication, was the white form, erect but helpless. For a long time we gazed without a word. At last, one more hardy than the rest said—"What can it be?"

What a question! What could it be but—Bubbles! Still, when the question was once asked, it did occur to one or two of us that possibly we might have jumped to a conclusion too hastily. It's wonderful how hardy a fellow will get when he's got twenty fellows clustering round him.

"He's alive, anyhow," said one. "Call out to him, some one," suggested another. "You're nearest the window, Fraser," said another. Fraser was vice-captain of the second fifteen, and always touchy whenever his pluck was called in question.

"I'm not afraid," he said, in a voice which was hardly quite steady. And as he spoke he threw up the window, and called out hurriedly, and in rather deferential tones—"Who are you down there?"

I don't suppose Fraser ever did a pluckier thing than ask that question. We listened, all ears, for the reply. But none came.

Talbot Baines Reed

Only a faint moan, as the apparition swayed uneasily towards us, and even seemed to try to raise itself in our direction; but never a word we heard, and we closed the window again as much in the dark as to its identity as ever.

What could we do? We couldn't go to bed with Bubbles's or anybody's ghost wandering about in the quadrangle below us, that was evident. But how were we to solve the mystery, unless indeed—

It was a terrible alternative, but the only one. We thought of it a good bit before any one proposed it. At last Fraser himself said—

"Who's game to come down into the quad?"

Fraser was on his mettle, or he would never have been so mad. At first a dead silence was the only answer to his challenge. Then Lamb said—

"I don't mind."

If he didn't mind, why should he nearly choke saying so? However, he broke the ice, and others followed. I considered myself as good a man as Lamb any day (it was only my own opinion), and I wasn't going to be outdone by him now. So I volunteered. And one or two others who considered themselves as good as I volunteered too, until the forlorn hope numbered a dozen.

"Come along," said Fraser, who had armed himself with a lighted candle and led the way.

I think those who stayed behind felt a little dismayed when the last of us glided from the door and left them behind.

Still, as far as happiness of mind was concerned, they would not have gained much had they been of our party. For we descended the staircase in rather depressed spirits, starting at every creak, and—some of us—wishing twenty times we were safe back in the dormitory. But there was no drawing back now.

What a noise the bars of the big door made as we unfastened them, and what an ominous shriek the lock gave as we turned the key! Our one hope was that the ghost would have taken fright and vanished before we reached the quadrangle. But no! As we stepped out into the damp breezy night the first thing that met our eyes was the distant, restless figure of Bubbles!

By one consent we halted, and as we did so a gust of wind extinguished our leader's candle! What was to be done? I glanced up, and saw the lights twinkling at the far distant dormitory window. Oh, whatever possessed me to come on this wild errand!

"Now then, you fellows!" It was Fraser's voice, and more like himself too. "Now then, stick all together and—"

"Better get a light first," suggested some one. "Will you run back to the dormitory and get the matches?" asked our leader.

Nothing more was said about the light.

We advanced a few yards, and then halted again.

"Better speak to him, I think," said Lamb.

"All right," said Fraser. "Now then, who are you? What's your name there?"

Talbot Baines Reed

His voice sounded loud and startling in the night air; but it was wasted breath. Never a word spoke Bubbles, but moaned as he struggled restlessly on the ground where he lay.

Fraser's spirits were rising every moment. "Oh, hang it!" he exclaimed. "I don't believe it's a ghost at all."

So saying, he made a further advance to within a few yards of the apparition.

If it wasn't a ghost, it was the most unearthly thing in the dark I ever saw as it lay there. We were still too far off to see it clearly, but it looked like some bloated creature without legs trying its hardest to rise on the feet that were not there.

"Do you hear?" shouted Fraser once more. "Why can't you speak and tell us who you are?"

The creature gave a long sigh by way of answer, but no more.

Fraser advanced another step, and we were preparing to follow, when the ghost slowly rose on end and made a sudden bound towards him!

In an instant we were back in the house, rushing pellmell up the stairs, and looking neither this way nor that till we were safe back in the dormitory with our companions.

We passed the remainder of that night dressed, and with candles burning, and it was not till morning broke that we dared once more look out of the window.

And then we discovered the mystery of Bubbles's ghost.

A small half-exhausted balloon, about five feet high, lay on the grass below, with enough gas in it still to toss about restlessly in the breeze, and now and then even to rise on end and drag its little car a few inches.

Where it came from and who it belonged to we never discovered. Probably some toy balloon let up by Christmas Eve revellers, who little thought it would alight on the roof of Jolliffe's, and after flopping about there for some minutes would finally tumble into the court below, and there act the part of Bubbles to a handful of scared schoolboys.

However, all's well that ends well, and among the many amusements which made that day a Merry Christmas to us all there was none over which we laughed more than "Bubbles's Ghost."

CHAPTER THREE

SUB-CHAPTER I

THE POETRY CLUB

During one of my terms at G—(and in speaking of that famous old school it is quite unnecessary to mention more than the first letter of its name) a serious epidemic broke out. It affected chiefly the lower half of the upper school, and during the brief period of its duration it assumed so malignant a type that it is still a marvel to me how any one of its victims ever survived it. The medical and other authorities were utterly incompetent to deal with it. In fact—incredible as it may seem—they deliberately ignored its existence, and left the sufferers to pull through as and how they could. Had it been an ordinary outbreak, as, for instance, scarlatina or diphtheria, or even measles, they would have cleared the school between two "call-overs," and had us all either in the infirmary or in four-wheelers at our parents' doors. But just because they had not got this—the most destructive kind of all epidemics—down on their list of infectious disorders, they chose to disregard it utterly, and leave us all to sink or swim, without even calling in the doctor to see us or giving our people at home the option of withdrawing us from our infected surroundings.

I love the old place too well to dwell further on this gross case of neglect. The present authorities no doubt would not repeat the error of their predecessors. Should they be tempted to do so, I trust the present harrowing revelation may be in time to avert the repetition of the calamity of which I was not only a witness but a victim.

The fact is, in the term to which I allude, we fellows in the upper Fifth and lower Sixth took to *writing poetry*! I don't know how the distemper broke out, or who brought it to G—. Certain it is we all took it, some worse than others; and had not the Christmas holidays happily intervened to scatter us and so reduce the perils of the contagion, the results might have been worse even than they were.

Now, one poet in a school is bad enough; and two usually make a place very uncomfortable for any ordinarily constituted person. But at G—it was not a case of one poet or even two. There were twenty of us, if there was one, and we each of us considered our claim to the laurel wreath paramount. Indeed, like the bards of old, we fell to the most unseemly contentions, and hated one another as only poets can hate.

It was my tragic lot to act as hon. secretary to the "Poetry Club," which constituted the hospital, so to speak in which our disease worked out its course during that melancholy term. Why they selected me, it is not for me to inquire. Some of my friends assured me afterwards that it was because, having no pretensions or even capacity to be a poet myself, I was looked upon as the only impartial member of our afflicted fraternity. No doubt they thought it a good reason. Had I known it at the time I should have repudiated the base insinuation with scorn. For I humbly conceived that I was a poet of the first water; and had indeed corrected a great many mistakes in Wordsworth and other writers, and written fifty-six or fifty-seven sonnets before ever the club was thought of. And Stray himself, who was accounted our Laureate, had only written thirty-four, and they averaged quite a line less than mine!

Be that as it may, I was secretary of the club, and to that circumstance the reader is indebted for the treat to which I am about to admit him. For in my official capacity I became custodian of not a few of the poetical aspirations of our members; and as, after the abatement of the disease, they none of them demanded back their handiwork—if poetry can ever be called handiwork—these effusions have remained in my charge ever since.

Some of them are far too sacred and tender for publication, and of others, at this distance of time, I confess I can make nothing at all. But there lies a batch before me which will serve as a specimen of our talents, and can hardly hurt the feelings of any one responsible for their production.

Our club, as I have said, was highly competitive in its operations. It by no means contented us each to follow his own course and woo his own muse. No, we all set our caps at the same muse and tried to cut one another out. If I happened to write an ode to a blackbird—and I wrote four or five— every one else must write an ode to a blackbird too; until the luckless songster must have hated the sound of its own name.

It was no easy work finding fit subjects for these poetic competitions. But the papers lying here before me remind me at least of one which excited great interest and keen rivalry. Complaints had been made that the club had hitherto devoted itself almost altogether to abstract rhapsodies, and had omitted the cultivation of itself in the epic or heroic side of its genius. On the other hand, the abstract rhapsodists protested that any one could write ballads, and that the subject to be chosen should at least be such as would admit of any treatment. One member suggested we should try the fifth proposition of the first book of Euclid, as being both abstract and historical—but he was deemed to be a scoffer. Eventually Stray said, why not take a simple nursery rhyme and work upon it, just as musicians take some simple melody as the theme of their great compositions?

It was a good idea, and after some consideration—for we had most of us forgotten our nursery rhymes—we fixed upon the tragical history of "Jack and Jill;" and decided to deal with it.

The understanding was that we might treat it any way we liked except—notable exception—in prose!

And so we went off to our studies and gave ourselves up to our inspirations. The result, the reader shall judge of for himself. Only he shall never know the real names of the poets; nor will anything induce me to disclose which particular production was the performance of the humble Author of this veritable narrative.

I will select the specimens haphazard, and distinguish them only by their numbers.

Number 1 was a follower of the classic models, and rendered the story in Homeric fashion.

> Attend, ye Nine! and aid me, while I sing
> The cruel fate of two whom heaven's dread king
> Hurled headlong to their doom. Scarce had the sun
> His blazing course for one brief hour run
> When Jack arose and radiant climbed the mount
> To where beneath the summit sprang the fount.
> Nor went he single; Jill, the beauteous maid,
> Danced at his side, and took his proffered aid.
> Together went they, pail in hand, and sang

Their love songs till the leafy valleys rang.
Alas! the fount scarce reached, the heedless swain
Turned on his foot and slipped and turned again.
Then fell he headlong: and the woe-struck maid,
Jealous of his fell doom, a moment stayed
And watched him; then to the depths she rushed
And shared his fate. Behold them, mangled, crushed.
Weep, oh my muse! for Jack, for Jill your tears outpour,
For hand-in-hand they'll climb the hill no more.

After this somewhat severe version of the story it is a relief
to turn to the lighter rendering of the same affecting theme
by Number 2. Number 2 was evidently an admirer of that
species of poetry which begins everything at the wrong end,
and seems to expect the reader to assist the poet in understanding what it is the latter is driving at.

What's the matter, Jack? Lost your head, poor wight!
I always told you the block wasn't screwed on too tight.
Tumbled? Is that it? It's a mercy you lit on your head.
Nothing brittle in that;—if you'd come on your feet
instead—
Broke it? No, never! You have? I knew it was slightly
cracked:
Never mind that there was nought to come out—that's a
comforting fact!
What! two of you? Who is the other? Not Jill, I declare!
Is her head cracked too? On my word, you're a pair.
Have I seen a pail lying about? Why, no, I have not.
Pails don't grow wild on this hill—that is, that I wot.
Oh, you dropped it, you did? Oh, I see, 'twas your pail,
And it tumbled you both o'er the rock? That's your tale.
It may turn up somewhere, perhaps. So you fell
Off the edge of the path that leads up to the well?
Well, all's well that ends well, at least so 'tis said;
But next time you'd better stay down, and try to fall

uphill instead.

Some of us at the time thought highly of this performance. I remember one fellow saying that Number 2 seemed to have caught the spirit of Mr Browning without his vagueness, which was a very great compliment.

Number 3's poetry ran chiefly in dramatic lines. He therefore boldly threw the narrative into dialogue form:—

Shepherdess.—Alas, my Jack is dead!

Shepherd.—I mourn for lovely Jill.

Both.—A common fate o'ertook them on the hill.

Shepherdess.—I watched them go—him and the hateful minx.

Shepherd.—I smiled to mark his footsteps on the brinks.

Both.—Cruel deceiver he/she! shameless intriguer she/he!

Shepherdess.—'Twas she who lured him o'er the cruel ledge.

Shepherd.—'Twas he who basely dragged her to the edge.

Both.—Oh! faithless he/she! oh! monstrous traitor she/he!

Shepherdess.—Her fate no tongue shall mourn, no eye shall weep; *Shepherd.*—His doom was all deserved upon the steep.

Both.—Oh! hapless he/she! oh! wicked wicked she/he!

Shepherdess.—Take warning, Shepherd; trust no faithless Jill.

Shepherd.—Nor you, fair nymph, with Jack e'er climb a hill.

Both.—Oh, woe is me! and woe, oh woe is thee!

Shepherdess.—With thee, poor youth, I fain would shed a tear.

Shepherd.—Maiden, with thee I'd sit and weep a year.

Both.—Wouldst thou but smile, I too would dry mine eye; Nay, let's do both, and laugh here till we cry.

Number 4 was a specimen of the simple ditty style which leaves nothing unexplained, and never goes out of its course for the sake of a well- turned phrase.

When Jack was twelve and Jill was ten
Their mother said, "My dear children,
I want you both to take the pail
We bought last week from Mr Gale,
And fill it full of water clear,
And don't be long away, do you hear?"
Then Master Jack and Sister Jill
Raced gaily up the Primrose Hill,
And filled the pail up to the top,
And tried not spill a single drop.
But sad to tell, just half way down
Jack tripped upon a hidden stone,
And tumbled down and cut his head
So badly that it nearly bled.
And Jill was so alarmed that she.
Let drop the pail immediately
And fell down too, and sprained her hand,
And had to go to Dr Bland
And get it looked to; while poor Jack
Was put to bed upon his back.

Number 4 regarded his performance with a certain amount of pride. He said it was after the manner of Wordsworth, and was a protest against the inflated style of most modern poetry, which seemed to have for its sole object to conceal its meaning from the reader. We had a good specimen of this kind of writing from Number 5, who wrote in blank verse, as he said, "after the German."

> I know not why—why seek to know? Is not
> All life a problem? and the tiniest pulse
> Beats with a throb which the remotest star
> Feels in its orbit? Why ask me? Rather say
> Whence these vague yearnings, whither swells this heart,
> Like some wild floweret leaping at the dawn?
> 'Tis not for me, 'tis not for thee to tell,
> But Time shall be our teacher, and his voice
> Shall fall unheard, unheeded in the midst!
> Still art thou doubtful? Then arise and sing
> Into the Empyrean vault, while I
> Drift in the vagueness of the Ambrosian night.

We none of us dared inquire of Number 5 what was the particular bearing of these masterly lines upon the history of Jack and Jill. I can picture the smile of pitying contempt with which such a preposterous question would have been met. And I observe by the figures noted at the back of this poem that it received very few marks short of the highest award.

Number 6 posed as democratic poet, who appealed to the ear of the populace in terms to which they are best accustomed.

> 'Twas a lovely day in August, at the top of Ludgate Hill
> I met a gay young couple, and I think I see them still;
> They were drinking at the fountain to cool their parching lips,
> And they said to one another, looking up between

their sips—

Chorus—I'd sooner have it hot, love; I'd rather have it
hot;
It's nicer with the chill off—much nicer, is it not?

They took a four-wheel growler for a drive all round the
town,
And told the knowing cabby not to let his *gee-gee* down;
But they'd scarcely got to Fleet Street when their off-hind-
wheel went bang,
And they pitched on to the kerb-stone, while the crowd
around them sang—

Chorus—I'm glad you've got it hot, love; I'm pleased
you've got it hot;
It's nicer with the chill off—much nicer, is it not?

Moral.

Now all you gay young couples, list to my fond appeal,
Beware of four-wheel growlers with spokes in their off-
hind-wheel;
And when you go up Ludgate Hill, all on a summer day,
Don't drink much at the fountain; or if you do, I say—
Be sure and take it hot, love; be sure and take it hot;
It's nicer with the chill off—much nicer, is it not?

This poem was not highly marked, although Number 6
confessed he had sat up all night writing it. He thought we
had missed the underlying philosophy of his version, and
was sorry for it. As he said, the first essential of a poem is
that it should be read, and he believed no one could deny that
he had at least written up to that requirement.

There was a more serious moral hidden in Number 7's version, which was stated to be on the models of the early sonnets:—

Two lovers on one common errand bound,
One common fate o'erwhelms; and so, me-seems,
A fable have we of our daily round,
Who in these groves of learning here are found
Climbing Parnassus' slopes. Our aim is one,
And one the path by which we strive to soar;
Yet, truer still, or ere the prize be won,
A common ruin hurls us to our doom.
'Twere best we parted, you and I; so, Fate,
Baulked of her double prey, may seek in vain,
And miss us both upon the shadowy plain.

The writer of Number 8 I always suspected of being a
borrower of other people's ideas. In fact it seemed as if he
must have had "A Thousand and One Gems" open before
him while he was at work, and to have drawn liberally from
its pages.

The way was long, the night was cold,
And Jack and Jill were young and bold.
"Try not the hill," the old man said,
"Dark lowers the tempest overhead."
A voice replied far up the height,
"We've many a step to walk this night."
Ah, luckless speech! ah, bootless boast!
Two minutes more and they were lost.
Who would not weep for Jack and Jill?
They died, though much against their will.
And the birds of the air all fell sobbing and sighing
As they heard of these two unfortunates dying.

The concluding line (which was the only original one in the
poem) was specially weak, and Number 8, I observe, only
received one vote, and that was probably given by himself.

Talbot Baines Reed

But, for originality and humour, Number 9's version was the most distinguished of the lot. With it I conclude, and if I may express an unbiassed opinion, many years after the memorable contest, I consider it far and away the best version of the story of Jack and Jill I have ever met with.

Jack and Jill
Went up a hill
To fetch a pail of water,
Jack fell down
And broke his crown,
And Jill came tumbling after.

CHAPTER FOUR

SUB-CHAPTER I

EIGHTEEN HOURS WITH A "KID"

[Copy of a holiday letter from Gus. Cutaway, of the Upper Remove, Shellboro', to his particular chum and messmate. Joseph Rackett]:—

Dear Jossy,—If you want a motto in life, I'll give you one— "'Ware kids!" Don't you have anything to do with kids, unless you want to lose all your pocket money, and be made a fool of before the fellows, and get yourself in a regular high old mess all round.

You needn't think I don't know what I'm talking about. I do. Promise you'll never say a word to anybody, especially to any of the fellows, and I'll tell you.

It was on breaking-up day. You know, all of you went off by the 2 train, and I had to wait till the 3:15. That's the worst of going through London; the trains never go at the right time. It came in up to time, for a wonder, and I bagged a second-class carriage to myself, and laid in some grub and a *B.O.P.* and made up my mind to enjoy myself.

Talbot Baines Reed

What do you think? Just as the bell was ringing, a female with a kid rushed on to the platform and made a dive for my carriage. I can tell you I was riled. But that wasn't half of it.

"Are you going to Waterloo, young gentleman?" asks the female, as out of breath as you like.

"Yes—why?" said I.

"Would you be so kind as to look after Tommy? His father will be there to meet him. He's got his ticket; haven't you, Tommy? Say 'Thank you' to the kind young gentleman. Bye, bye; be a good boy."

"Right forward," sings out the guard.

"Love to daddy," says the female.

"Stand away from the train," shouts the porter.

And then we were off. And here was I, left alone in a carriage with a kid called Tommy, that I was to give over to a chap called daddy at Waterloo!

How would *you* have liked it yourself, Jossy? I was awfully disgusted. And, of course, till the train was off, I never thought of saying, "I can't," and then it was too late. I can tell you it's a bit rough on a fellow to be served that way. If ever you're going by train and see a female and a kid coming along, hop out of the carriage till you see which carriage they get into; and then go and get into another.

I made up my mind I'd leave the little cad to himself, so I started to read. At least I pretended to. Really I took a good squint at him while he wasn't looking. He was a kid of about four and a half, I fancy, with a turnippy head and a suit of togs that must have been new, he was so jolly proud of them. He sat staring at the lamp and swinging his legs for a good bit. Then he got hold of the window-strap and fooled about with that. Then he remembered his swagger togs and looked himself all over, and stuck his hands in his pocket. He twigged me looking at him as he did so.

"I've got a knife," he said, as cool as if he'd known me a couple of terms.

"Who said you hadn't?" I responded.

"It's in my pocket," he said.

"Oh," said I. I didn't want to encourage him.

He pulled it out, staring at me all the time. Then he slipped down off the seat and brought it up to me.

"Open it," he said.

"Open it yourself," said I.

"I can't," said he. "Open it! Open it!"

"All right, keep your temper," said I, and I opened it. A beastly blunt thing it was. "There you are; take it."

"I want to sit beside you," he said, when he'd got it.

"Do you? I don't want you. Haven't you got all the rest of the carriage?"

"Lift Tommy up," he whined.

I'd a good mind to chuck him out of the window.

"Lift yourself up," I said, "and shut up. I want to read." Then I'm bothered if the young cad didn't begin yelling! Just because I didn't lift him up. I never saw such a blub-baby in all my life. I couldn't make out what he was up to at first. I thought he was curtseying and seeing how long he could hold his breath. But when it did come out, my eye! I thought the engine-driver would hear. I was in a regular funk; I thought he'd got a fit or something; I never heard such yelling. He was black in the face over it, and dancing. I'd a good mind to pull the cord and stop the train. But I thought I'd see if I could pull him round first.

So I picked him up and stuck him up on the seat. Would you believe it, Jossy? The moment he was up he stopped howling and began grinning. It had all been a plant to get me to lift him up; and as soon as he'd made me do it he laughed at me!

I can tell you it's not pleasant to be made a fool of, even by a kid.

"I'm sitting beside you now," he said, as much as to tell me he'd scored one off me.

I was too disgusted to take any further notice of him. I suppose he saw I was riled, and began to be a bit civil. He pulled a nasty sticky bit of chocolate out of his pocket and held it up to my nose.

"A sweetie for you," he said.

I didn't want to have him yelling again, so I took it. Ugh!— all over dust and hairs, and half melted.

He watched me gulp it down, and then, to my relief, got hold of the *Boy's Own Paper* and began looking at the pictures. He got sick of that soon, and went and looked out of the window. Then he came and sat by me again, and began to get jolly familiar. He stroked my cheeks with his horrid sticky hand, and then climbed up on the seat and tried to lark with my cap. Then just because I didn't shut him up, he clambered up on my back and nearly throttled me with his arms round my neck; and—what do you think?—he began to kiss me!

That was a drop too much.

"Stow it, kid!" I said.

"Dear, dear!" he said, getting regularly maudlin, and kissing me at about two a second.

"Let go, do you hear? you're scrugging me."

"Nice mannie," he said.

I didn't know what to do until I luckily thought of my grub.

"Like a bun?" said I.

He let me go and was down beside me like a shot. You should have seen him walk into that bun! His face was all over it, and the crumbs were about an inch deep all over the place. When he got near the end of bun Number 1, he looked up as near choking as they make them, and said—

"I like buns awfully."

"All right, have another," said I. You see as his governor was going to meet him in town, it didn't matter much to me if he got gripes at night. Anything to keep him quiet.

After the third bun he was about full up, and said he was

　　　　　　　　Talbot Baines Reed

thirsty. I couldn't make the young ass understand that I had no water in the carriage. He kept on saying he was thirsty for half an hour, till we came to a station. I had made up my mind I would get into another carriage at the first stop we came to; but, somehow, it seemed rather low to leave the kid in the lurch. So I bought him a glass of milk instead, which set him up again. Nobody else got in the carriage—knew better—and off we went again.

He'd got an awful lot to say for himself; about dicky-birds and puff- puffs, and dogs, and trouser-pockets and rot of that sort, and didn't seem to care much whether I listened or no. Then, just when I thought he had about run dry and was getting sleepy, he rounded on me with—

"Tell me a story."

"Me? I don't know any stories."

"Oh yes; a funny one, please."

"I tell you I don't know any—what about?"

"'The Three Bears.'"

"I don't know anything about 'three bears,'" said I.

"Do! do!! do!!!" he said, beginning to get crusty.

So I did my best. He kept saying I was all wrong, and putting me right; he might just as well have told it himself. I told him so. But he took no notice, and went on badgering me for more stories.

I can tell you I was getting sick of it!

When I made up a story for him to laugh at, he looked so solemn and said—

"Not that; a funny one."

And when I told him a fairy tale, he snapped up and said he didn't like it.

It ended in my telling him the "The Three Bears" over and over again. It was about the sixty-fifth time of telling that we got to Vauxhall, and had to give up tickets.

"Now, young 'un, look out for your governor when we get in—I don't know him, you know."

The young ass didn't know what I meant.

"Look out for daddy, then," I said.

He promptly stuck his head out of the window and said the ticket- collector was daddy; then that the porter was; then that a sweep on the platform was.

It wasn't very hopeful for spotting the real daddy at Waterloo. I told him to shut up and wait till we got there.

When we got there, I stuck him up at the window, as large as life, for his governor to see. There were a lot of people about; but I can tell you I was pretty queer when no one owned him. We hung about a quarter of an hour, asking everybody we met if they'd come to meet a kid, and watching them all go off in cabs, till we had the platform to ourselves.

"Here's a go, kid!" said I; "daddy's not come."

"I 'spex," says he, "when the middling-size bear found his porridge eaten up, he wondered who it was."

"Shut up about the bears," said I. "What about your gov.— your daddy? Where does he live?"

"In London town," said he, as soon as I could knock those bears out of his head.

"Whereabouts? What street?"

"London town."

"Do you mean to say—look here, what's your name? Tommy what?"

"It's Tommy," he said.

"I know that. Is it Tommy Jones, or Tommy Robinson, or what?"

"It's Tommy," he repeated. "My name's Tommy." Here was a nice go! Stranded with a kid that didn't know his own name, or where his governor lived! The worst of it was, I had to stop in London that night as there was no train on. My pater had written to get a room for me at the Euston Hotel, so that I should be on the spot for starting home first train in the morning.

I was regularly stumped, I can tell you. It never turned a feather on the kid, his governor not turning up; and I couldn't make the idiot understand anything. He hung on to me singing and saying, "Who's been tasting my porridge and eaten it all up?" or else cheeking the porters, or else trying to whistle to make the trains go.

I thought I'd better leave word with the station-master where I'd gone, in case any one turned up; and then there was nothing for it but to take a cab across to the hotel.

The kid was no end festive to have a ride in the cab. It would have been in a little better taste if he'd held his tongue, and shown a little regret for the jolly mess he'd let me into. But, bless you, he didn't care two straws.

"What will daddy say when he can't find you?" I said, trying to get him to look at things seriously.

"Daddy will say, 'Who's been sitting in my chair, and broken the bottom out?'" said he, still harping on those blessed bears. I gave him up after that, and let him jaw on.

When we got to the hotel I was in another fix. The chap in charge said he'd got instructions about one young gentleman, but not two.

"Oh, I'm looking after this boy," said I, "till tomorrow: I'll have him in my room."

The chap looked as if he didn't like it. And, of course, just when he was thinking it over, the young cad must go and cheek him.

"What makes that ugly man so red on his nose?" he asks at the top of his voice, for every one to hear.

The chap was no end riled at that, and looked as if he'd kick us out. When he'd cooled down he said—

"You wait here; I'll attend to you presently."

That was a nice go! If I had had tin enough I should have

gone somewhere else; but I'd only got enough for the journey to-morrow, and so thought I'd better hang on here, where the governor had arranged.

The lid went on anyhow while we were waiting in the hall. He ran and stood in front of people, and he pulled waiters' coat-tails, and got mixed up with the luggage, and called out to me to know where the ugly red-nosed man had gone. At last I had to pull him in.

"Look here, kid!" said I; "if you don't hold your jaw and sit here quietly, I'll give you to a policeman."

"Tell me about the bears, then."

Oh, how I loathed those bears! Think of me, captain of my eleven, in that rackety hall, with people coming and going, and a row enough to deafen you, telling a kid about The Three Bears! You may grin, Jossy; but I was reduced to it.

After a time the hotel chap came and said we were to have a double- bedded room, and he should charge half-extra for the kid, and if we wanted dinner we'd better look sharp, as it was just beginning.

So we went up and washed—at least I had to wash the kid's sticky hands and face for him—and then came down to *table d'hote*. I was in a regular funk lest any of our fellows, or any one I knew, should see me. We got squeezed in between a lady in grand evening dress, and a professor chap with blue spectacles; and as they were both attending to their neighbours, I hoped we might scrape through without a scene.

You should have seen that kid tuck in! I mildly suggested that he'd better not have any mock-turtle soup; but he began to get up steam for a bowl and a half, so I gave it up.

He said it was ugly stuff, but for all that he polished off a plate of it, and then walked into salmon. After that he had a turn at roast pork and apple sauce, and after that a cabinet pudding and some Gorgonzola cheese. He was very anxious to have some beer, like the professor, or some wine, like the lady; but I put my foot down there, and let him have lemonade instead. You should have seen people stare at him! The professor glared as if he was a rum animal.

"Your brother?" said he.

"Not exactly," said I.

"Uncommon appetite. Would you mind telling me in the morning what sort of night he had? I shall be curious to know."

The lady glared too, chiefly because the kid had sprinkled her silk dress with melted butter, and pork gravy and lemonade. He caught her eye once, and said out loud to her—

"Our cat's called Flossy; what's your cat called?"

The lady turned away; whereupon the kid began his cheek again.

"That lady," said he to me and the company at large, "has got a nice dress and a nasty face. I like nice faces bestest—do you?"

"Shut up, or I'll clout your ear," snarled I, in a regular perspiration of disgust.

"What's clout?" inquired he. Then, feeling his ears, "My ears don't stick out like that man's over there, do they?"

Talbot Baines Reed

"Do you hear? shut up, you little fool!"

"We've got a donkey at home, and his—"

Here I could stand it no longer, and lugged him off, whether he liked it or no. He was just as bad in the reading-room. He wouldn't sit still unless I told him stories, and made a regular nuisance of himself to the other people. Then (I suppose it was his big feed) he began to get crusty, and blubbered when I talked sharply to him, and presently set up a regular good old howl.

"Why don't you put the child to bed?" said a lady; "he's no business up at this hour."

Nice, wasn't it?

I had to sneak off with him upstairs, howling all the way. He wouldn't stop till I gave him a mild cuff on the head. That seemed to bring him round enough to demand the "The Three Bears" once more.

Anything to keep him still; so at it I went again.

Then I told him to go to bed; and he told me to undress him, as he couldn't do the buttons.

I can't make out how I got him out of his togs. Then he kicked up no end of a shine because I was going to stick him in bed without his bath.

"I've got no bath," said I; "wait till the morning."

"Tommy wants his bath. Bring it! bring it!!" he shrieked.

Finally I had to mess him about in a basin in cold water,

which set him yelling worse than ever. Then I had to put him in my night-gown, for he'd got none of his own.

"I want to get in beside you," he said, as I stuck him in bed.

"I'm not going to bed yet," said I; "not likely, at eight o'clock!"

More yells; and a chambermaid came and knocked at the door to know what was the matter.

I tried all I knew to quiet him down. He wouldn't listen to me, not even when I tried to tell him his "Three Bears." He bellowed out one incessant "Want to get in beside you! Want to get in beside you!!" till finally I chucked up the sponge and actually went to bed to oblige him.

He simmered down after that; and I began to hope he'd drop off and get to sleep. But bless you, Jossy, was it likely, after those buns and the dinner he'd had?

We had a fearful night, I can tell you. He kicked till I was black and blue, and rolled over and over till I hadn't a stitch on me. Then he wanted some water to drink. Then he wanted the gas alight. Then he began to blubber for his mother. Then he wanted the clothes on. Then he wanted them off. Then he got his feet entangled in the night-gown. Then he wanted some chocolates. Then he wanted to know who was talking in the next room. Then he wanted the pillow turned over. Then he wanted a story told him, and shut me up before I'd begun one sentence of it. Then he wanted me to put my arm round him. Then he wanted me to lie over on the edge of the bed. Then he had a pain in his "tummy," and called on me to make it well, and howled because I couldn't.

Poor little beggar! He was in a jolly bad way, and I couldn't

Talbot Baines Reed

well cut up rough; but I can tell you it was the worst night I ever spent. He didn't quiet down till about three in the morning; and then he went off with his head on my chest and his hand on my nose, and I daren't for the life of me shift an inch, for fear of bringing it all on again.

I suppose I must have dropped off myself at last; for the next thing I remember, it was broad daylight, and the young cad was sitting on the top of me as merry as a cricket, trying to prize my eyes open with his fingers.

"Can't you let a chap be?" grunted I; "haven't you made a beast enough of yourself all night without starting again now?"

"I want to see your eyes," said he.

Then he began to jump up and down on the top of me, and explained that he was "riding in the puff-puff."

I wished to goodness he was! Of course I had to wake up, and then we had those brutal "Three Bears" on again for an hour, till it was time to get up.

He insisted on being tubbed all over, with soap, and criticised me all the while.

"Boys who spill on the carpet must be whipped," said he. "Mother will whip you, and you'll cry—ha, ha!"

"I don't care," said I, "as long as she clears you off."

He never seemed to understand what I said, and wasn't a bit set down by this.

Then came the same old game of getting him into his togs,

and parting his horrid hair, and blowing his nose, and all that.

I can tell you I was about sick of it when it was done.

When we got down in the hall, the first chap we met was the hotel man.

"There's the ugly man with the red nose," sings out the kid. "I can see him—there is he!" pointing with all his might.

"Look here, young gentleman," said the man, coming to me, "we aren't used to be kept awake all night by your noise or your baby's. You may tell your papa he needn't send you here again. There's half a dozen of my visitors leaving to-day, because they couldn't get a wink of sleep all night."

"No more could I," said I.

He was going to say something more, but just then a man came in from the street. Directly he spotted the kid, he rushed up to him.

"Why, it *is* Tommy," said he.

Tommy put on a grin, and dug his hands into his pockets. "I've got a knife," said he, "of my very own."

"Are you the young gentleman who left the message at Waterloo?" said the man. "Why, the letter I got said the train got in at 8 a.m., not 8 p.m. You don't know what a turn it gave me to go down there this morning and not see him. Have you had him here all night?"

"Rather," said I.

Talbot Baines Reed

"Daddy, there's an ugly man came to this house. I can see him now, with a red nose. Look there!"

"I hope he's been a good boy," said the proud father. "I'm sure I'm much obliged. I'm afraid he's been a trouble to you. I've got a cab here. My word, I'm glad I've got you safe, Tommy, my boy. Come, say good-bye to the kind gentleman."

"He was naughty, and spilt the water on the floor. He must be whipped—ha, ha!" observed Tommy, by way of farewell.

He didn't seem to care twopence about leaving me, and chucked me up for his governor as if I'd been a railway porter. However, I can tell you I was glad to see the back of him, and didn't envy his governor a little bit.

Of course, I'd lost my first train home, and had to wait till mid-day, to endure the scowls of the hotel man, and the frowns of all the people who had been kept awake by the kid's row. Among others there was the professor.

"Well," said he, "what sort of night did baby have?"

"Middling," said I.

"I expected it would be middling," said he.

Now, Jossy, you know what I mean by "'Ware kids." Keep all this mum, whatever you do. I wouldn't have any of the fellows hear about it for the world. I can tell you, I feel as if I deserve a week's holiday longer than the rest of you. Never you utter the words "Three Bears" in my hearing, or there'll be a row.

Yours truly, Gus. Cutaway.

CHAPTER FIVE

SIGURD THE HERO

SUB-CHAPTER I

THE TOWER OF THE NORTH-WEST WIND

On the rugged shore of the Northern Sea, where the summer sun never sets, there stood long ago a grim bleak fortress, called the Tower of the North-West Wind. Before it stretched the sea, which thundered ceaselessly at its base, like a wolf that gnaws at the root of some noble oak. On either side of it glittered the blue fiord, dotted with numberless islets, throwing its long arms far inland. Behind it frowned a dense forest of pines as far as eye could reach, in which the wind roared day and night, mingled often with the angry howls of the wolves.

The Tower of the North-West Wind stood there, the solitary work of man in all that wild landscape. Not a sign of life was to be seen besides. Not even a fisherman's hut on the shores of the fiord, or a woodman's shed among the trees. The stranger might easily have taken the rugged pile itself for a part of the black cliff on which it stood. No road seemed to lead up to it, no banner floated from its walls, no trumpet startled the sea-birds that lodged amongst its turrets.

Yet the old castle was not the deserted place it looked, for here dwelt Sigurd, the mightiest hero of all that land, brother to Ulf, the king.

Men hated Ulf as much as they loved his brother; for Sigurd, with all his prowess, was just and generous, and lied to no man.

"If Sigurd were but king," said they one to the other, "our land would be the happiest the sun shines upon. As it is, Ulf makes us wretched. We had rather be his enemies than his friends."

But though they said this one to another, Sigurd listened to none of it, and when they urged him to rebel, he sternly bade them hold their peace. And he went forth and fought the battles of the king, his brother, and they followed him, wishing only the battle-cry were "Sigurd!" and not "Ulf!"

For all this loyalty the king gave his brother little thanks. Indeed, as victory followed victory, and Sigurd's fame rose higher and higher, Ulf's heart swelled with jealousy, and jealousy presently grew to hate. For it was not in Ulf's nature to endure that another should be held greater than himself. So, instead of rewarding his brother for his service, he accused him and degraded him, and made another general in his place.

"Now," said the soldiers, "our chief will surely rebel, and we will follow his lead, and pluck down Ulf from the throne and set up our Sigurd."

But Sigurd sternly silenced them, and bade them serve their king as they feared him. He meanwhile departed sadly from his brother's court, and came and dwelt alone in his Tower of the North-West Wind.

For many weeks the time passed slowly, as Sigurd brooded over his wrongs and pined in idleness.

Yet this grieved him less than the secret visits of not a few of his old comrades, who had deserted Ulf, and now came begging him to lead them forth and rid the land of a tyrant. He sent them each sternly away, bidding them, on pain of his anger, return to their duty and serve the king; and they durst not disobey.

So passed many a weary month in the Tower of the North-West Wind, when one bright summer day a little fleet of English ships sailed gaily up the fiord under the castle walls.

Sigurd joyfully bade the voyagers welcome to his castle, for the chief of the little band was Raedwald, an English king, whom Sigurd himself only two years before had visited in his own land. There, too, he had met not Raedwald only, but Raedwald's beautiful daughter, who now, with her gay train of attendants, accompanied her father on this visit to his friend and comrade.

And now the days passed gaily and only too swiftly for the happy Sigurd. In the company of Raedwald and amid the smiles of the ladies, Ulf was forgotten, and all the wrongs of the past vanished. The Tower of the North-west Wind was no longer a gloomy fortress, but a gay palace, and, like the summer day in the northern heavens, the sun of Sigurd's content knew no setting.

Before the day of Raedwald's departure arrived a wedding had taken place in the chapel of the good old Tower, and the English king, as he hauled his anchors and set his sails westward, knew not whether to mourn over the daughter he had given up or to rejoice over the son he had gained.

As for Sigurd, he could do nothing but rejoice, and some who saw him and heard him laugh said, smiling—

"The queen his wife is a fairer sweetheart than was the king his brother. Ulf and our country and all of us are forgotten in the smiles of this little English maiden."

But three days after Raedwald had sailed a storm broke over the Tower of the North-West Wind. The summer sea lashed furiously against the rocks, and far up the fiord the angry breakers rushed in, so that no boat could live upon their surface for an hour.

That night as Sigurd sat heedless of the hurricane without and feasted with his lords and ladies, they came and told him that a raft had been driven ashore at the foot of the castle, with a man upon it half dead. Sigurd bade them instantly bring him to the castle, and give him fire and clothing and food, to revive him in his unhappy plight.

This they did, and presently came to the hero with the hews that the man lived and desired to speak with his deliverer. So Sigurd ordered him to be brought up. And as the tempest raged without, his heart rejoiced to know that one man at least had been saved from its ravages.

The man was of the common order, and though clothed in a rough woodman's suit it was plain to see he was a soldier.

He fell at the feet of the prince and poured forth his thanks for the shelter given him that night.

"And who art thou?" asked Sigurd, to whom such thanks

were never welcome.

"I am a servant of King Ulf thy brother."

At the mention of the king's name the faces of those present fell, and Sigurd asked, sternly—

"And what is thy errand here?"

"I was sent," said the man, "with two others, to spy into your state here. The king has heard of your merrymakings and of your alliance with the English king. He bade us see how you were armed and how prepared for a sudden assault, and then return secretly and report it to him."

"And is it thus you perform your errand?" cried Sigurd. "Where are thy companions?"

"Drowned, my liege, in the fiord, as I had been but for your gracious help."

"And when is the king coming to assault this tower?" demanded an English noble who sat near.

"Never," said the man, shortly.

"And why?" asked Sigurd.

"Oh, my liege," said the man, dropping once more on his knees, "please Heaven, in a week's time there will be no king in all this land but Sigurd."

The hero started from his seat and seized the man roughly.

"What is it you say?" he cried. "Speak out, and that plainly, or it will be worse for you!"

Talbot Baines Reed

"On this day week," said the trembling serf, "Ulf is to visit his castle of Niflheim. He goes there alone, as you, my liege, came hither, to receive his bride. But he will never return the way he came, for Bur and Harald, your friends, my prince, have vowed to slay him there, and at one blow rid the land of a tyrant and give it a just and good king."

When Sigurd heard this he turned white and red with wrath and fear. Fiercely he summoned his guards, and bade them seize the spy and cast him into the dungeon.

Then, as soon as words came, he turned to the company and said—

"You hear what this knave says?"

"Yes, we hear," cried some, "and we rejoice that Sigurd's day has come at last. Long live King Sigurd!"

Then Sigurd struck the table with his fist as he started to his feet and glared at the rash companions.

"Villains!" he shouted, with a voice that made the room itself tremble. "Yes, Sigurd's day has come—the day for teaching cowards like you the duty of a knight and a brother. Ulf, at his bridal, unarmed, slain by traitors' hands. Is that the chivalry ye praise? If so, begone from my sight and reach of this arm! But 'tis no time for talk. Without there, my arms! and saddle my horse!"

"What means this!" cried all. "Where go you, Sigurd?"

"I go to my brother," he said.

"Your brother! Ulf is eight days' sail from here!"

"'Tis but five days across the forest," said the hero.

At this the ladies shrieked, and all looked on Sigurd as a man that is mad.

"The forest, said you?" cried one. "It swarms with wolves, Sigurd, and where the wolves are not, the robbers lurk."

Sigurd smiled scornfully. "It is wolves and robbers I go to seek," he said.

"If thou wilt go," they said then, "we will go with thee."

"No!" cried Sigurd. "I go alone. Let him who loves me remain here and guard my lady. I can trust you to be true to a lady—but ye have yet to learn to be loyal to a prince."

At this many hung their heads and were silent.

Sigurd meanwhile put on his armour, and turned hurriedly to bid farewell to his wife. The hero's voice trembled as he prayed Heaven to guard over her.

They all accompanied him to the courtyard, where, quickly mounting, he departed, and rode slowly forward into the forest.

Sigurd rode slowly forward into the forest, and as he entered it he turned for one last look at the brave old castle which held within its walls the joy of his life—and a soft voice at his ear whispered "Return!"

Yet he halted not, nor did his courage waver, for another voice, louder than the other, cried "Onward!" It seemed like his brother's voice, as he had known it years ago, before troubles came, and when as merry boys the two lived with but one heart between them. And at the sound he put spurs to his horse and plunged into the wood.

Gloomy indeed was this forest of lonely pines, which rocked and groaned in the wind, and in which a dim twilight deepening often into black darkness reigned on every hand. And gloomier still were those distant cries which rose ever and again above the tempest, and caused even the brave horse to shiver as he heard them.

But Sigurd shivered not, but rode forward, trusting in his God and listening only to that old-remembered voice ahead.

For a league the road was easy and the perils few. For thus far the woodman's axe had often fallen amidst the thick underwood, clearing a path among the trees and driving before it the sullen wolves into the deeper recesses of the forest.

But as Sigurd rode on, and the boughs overhead closed in between him and the light of day, these few traces of man's hand vanished.

His good horse stumbled painfully over the tangled ground, often hardly finding himself a path among the dense trunks. And all around, those wild yells which had mingled with the tempest seemed to draw closer, as though eagerly awaiting the horse and its rider somewhere not far off.

Sigurd heeded them not, but cheered himself as he rode on by calling to mind some of the beautiful stories of the old religion of his land. He thought of the elves and fairies who were said to dwell in these very forests, and at midnight to creep up from their hiding-places and gambol and play tricks among the flowers and dewdrops with the wild bees and the summer insects, or dance in magic circles on the greensward.

And it did his heart good to feel he was not alone, but that these merry little companions were with him, lightening his way and guiding his course all the night through. And he thought too of luckless dwarfs whom Odin had condemned to dig and delve all day deep in the ground, and throw fuel on the great central fire of the earth, but who at night, like the fairies, might come above and revisit then old haunts. And even these mischievous little companions helped to cheer the heart of the wayfarer and beguile his journey.

And so he plodded on all through the night, resolutely plunging deeper and deeper into the forest, and leaving the Tower of the Norths Waistcoat Wind league after league farther behind.

The day passed as the night had passed. Save for an occasional halt to rest his horse and refresh his body with food, nothing broke the dullness of the journey. The wolves alone were silent, waiting for the night. As the afternoon wore on Sigurd could see their gaunt forms skulking among the trees, casting many a hungry sidelong glance that way, and licking their cruel jaws as foretaste of the wished-for meal.

And now Sigurd needed to stop his ears closer than ever against the voice which cried "Return!" and set his face still more steadfastly towards Niflheim. For though his heart never faltered, his spirits drooped as another night closed in, and weary and oppressed he pushed onward.

The fairies no longer cheered him, nor could he smile again at the antics of the dwarfs. The soft voice of one behind was all he heard, and the music of its tones was sad. The voice before still cried "Onward," but it mingled dismally with the storm overhead and the wild and ever-increasing howling of the wolves. The horse, too, seemed to share his master's

Talbot Baines Reed

trouble, for he stumbled forward spiritlessly, hanging his head and trembling at each approaching howl.

Nearer and nearer those cruel voices closed in around him, not one but half a score. Stealthily at first they dogged their prey. Then, gaining boldness, advanced, and pressed more closely on the heels of the horse. Sigurd, as he glanced quickly round, saw a score of cruel eyes flash out in the darkness, and almost felt the hot breath in his face.

One bolder than the rest made an angry snap at the horse's heel. The unhappy animal, who long ere this had lost his wonted nerve, made a sudden bound forward, which almost unhorsed his rider. The sudden movement was the signal for the pack to leap forward with wild yells, and next moment Sigurd and his gallant horse were fighting for dear life.

Desperately fought Sigurd, swinging his trusty axe right and left, and carrying at each stroke death among his savage assailants.

At length the horse, beset on all sides, exhausted, wounded, dropped to the ground, unable longer to hold out. With a cry of savage triumph the wolves leapt upon him in a hideous, howling, struggling mass. Sigurd, scarcely gaining his feet after the fall, started forward alone. For the horse that was dead was more to the wolves than the hero who yet lived. And over the carcass they jostled and fought, and screamed ravenously, till nought remained to fight for.

Sigurd knew well, as he hastened forward, axe in hand and sword in belt—his spear had broken off short—that the respite was but short. A few minutes and the pack would be once more on the trail, and then it would be his turn. Yet he prayed his God to send him help and bring him through the peril.

He hurried on, yet slowly, by reason of the tangled paths and dense underwood of the forest, listening to the angry tumult behind and wondering how long before the hue and cry began once more.

It was not long. Scarcely had he forced his way a half-mile when he could hear the pack following. Onward they came at a rush with hideous tumult, and Sigurd knew that the foremost would be upon him in a moment. He strode on, casting a glance back at every step, and gripping fast his trusty axe. Presently, just as he reached a small clearing among the trees, the brushwood behind him crackled, and a pair of eyes gleamed close at hand.

Then Sigurd turned, and putting his back against a broad tree, waited.

On they came, half sated, doubly savage with the taste of blood on their jaws.

Desperately once more fought Sigurd, swinging his axe right and left and dealing death at every blow, till he stood surrounded by a half-circle of dead or dying wolves.

Sigurd fought till he could scarce stand or wield his axe. Many a cruel wound weakened him, his eyes grew dim, his hand unsteady, his blows uncertain. He could do no more. The axe fell from his grasp, and he reeled back.

As he did so there rose, loud above the wind and above the howling of the wolves, a cry which caused Sigurd to start once more to his feet, and the wild beasts to pause midway in their mortal onslaught.

It was the deep-mouthed voice of a dog, and next moment a huge mastiff dashed from out of the thicket and fastened on

Talbot Baines Reed

the throat of the foremost wolf.

It was Sigurd's own watch-dog Thor, whom some dear hand had loosed from his chain and sent forth into the forest to guard and maybe save his master.

At the sight of the great champion, and at sound of his bark, the cowardly wolves one by one slunk sullenly back into the woods, and Sigurd felt that he was saved.

A joyous meeting was that between gallant master and gallant hound.

"Thor, my brave dog," cried Sigurd, "is it to thee, then, I owe my life—my brother's life? Yet not to thee so much as to the fair lady who sent thee, a messenger of love and life to me. Thanks, Thor, thanks lady, thank most to God. Now shall I reach Niflheim even yet."

Thor wagged his great tail and barked joyfully in answer.

All that night Sigurd lay secure, watched over by the sleepless Thor, whose honest bark was the sweetest music that ever lulled a hero to repose.

For two days Sigurd trudged safely onward through that dense forest, with Thor, the dog, beside him. The way was hard and painful, and the hero's limbs, now his only support, crashed wearily through the thickets. But, faint and weary though he was, his bold heart and the thought of his brother carried him through.

Four days had come and gone since he quitted the Tower of the North-West Wind, and in three more Ulf would either be saved or slain. Sigurd, as he thought of it, strode sternly forward and shut his ears to all the backward voices.

And, with Thor at his side, all danger from the wolves seemed at an end. As the two pressed on many a distant how! fell on their ears, many a gaunt form stole out from among the trees to gaze at them, and then steal back. Thor's honest bark carried panic among those cruel hordes, while it comforted the heart of Sigurd.

For two days, without sleep, without rest, without proper food, the hero walked on, till, on the fifth morning after quitting his castle, the light broke in among the trees, the woodman's cheerful axe resounded through the glades, the angry howling sounded far behind, and Sigurd knew he was on the other side of the forest.

In one day he would reach Jockjen, and scarce two hours' march beyond Jockjen lay Niflheim.

Thor seemed to guess his master's mind, and with a hopeful bark bounded forward. But Sigurd regarded his companion sadly and doubtfully. He called him to him, caressed him lovingly, and said—

"Good Thor, thou hast been like a messenger from God to bring me through this wood. Alas! that we must part."

Thor stopped short as he heard these last words, and moaned piteously.

"Yes, good Thor," said the hero, sadly, "for I cannot live another day without sending a message to my lady that I am safe, thanks to her and thee."

The dog, who seemed to understand it all, looked up in his master's face beseechingly, as if to persuade him against his resolve.

Talbot Baines Reed

"The danger now is past," said Sigurd. "No wolves haunt the forest betwixt here and Jockjen, and in the town thy presence may discover me. So haste back, good Thor, to my lady with this my message."

So saying he took from the ground a smooth strip of bark, on which, with the point of his sword, he wrote something. Then, turning to Thor, "Carry this," he said, "to her."

And as Thor turned and hastened off on his errand, Sigurd looked after him and sighed, and wished he too were going that way.

But time forbade that he should linger long thus, and once more he turned his face resolutely towards Jockjen and went on alone.

Although the forest stretched some leagues farther, the trees were no longer dense or the path difficult. In parts large clearings had been made, and felled timber here and there betokened the busy hand of the woodman. Sigurd met more than one of these, who accosted him. He would not, however, tarry with any of them, but pressed eagerly forward, so that they would turn and look after this noble knight and wonder who he was, and whither he hasted.

One of these simple folk with whom he waited a few minutes to partake of a hasty meal said, at parting—

"Beware, my lord, of the robbers who haunt the skirts of the forest. They come suddenly upon the unwary traveller, and have no pity."

Sigurd smiled.

"I have passed the four-footed wolves," he said; "I fear not the two- footed."

"Nay, but," said the peasant, "they are not to be despised. Ever since Sigurd was banished many of his soldiers have deserted the king, and now live the robber's life in these woods. Stay here, my lord, till a band of us will be going to Jockjen together."

But Sigurd smiled scornfully, and, thanking the man, started forward, fearing nothing save arriving too late at Niflheim.

Yet the woodman's warning was not lost upon him, for he walked with his drawn sword in his hand, keeping both his eyes and ears open as he went.

All that day he pressed onward, and towards evening came to a lonely part of the wood, where the trees for a short space all round closed thickly overhead and shut out the light. He had passed through this spot, and was once more emerging into the open, when three men suddenly sprang out of the thicket and faced him.

Two of them were in the garb of common peasants, and carried, the one a club, the other a knife. Sigurd guessed them at once to be two of the robbers of whom the woodman had warned him. Their companion was a powerful man in the dress of a soldier, and carried a sword. In him, though he knew not the man, Sigurd recognised a soldier of the army of the king, who, as he might guess, had deserted his lawful calling for the life of a bandit.

The party was plainly unprepared to meet a knight fully armed. They had expected rather to find some defenceless merchant, or even woodman, whom they might easily overcome and as easily rob.

They fell back an instant before the noble form of Sigurd, but the next, true to their calling, rushed upon him, shouting to him to surrender and yield up whatever of value he might possess on his person.

Sigurd wasted not a word in replying to this insolent challenge, but defended himself against the sudden assault. At the first onslaught the two bandits were foremost, who thought to bear him down by sheer weight. But Sigurd, stepping back a pace, caught the knife of the one on his shield, while with his own sword he ran his comrade through the body. So quickly was it done, that the soldier, advancing wildly to the attack, stumbled and fell over the body of the prostrate man; and before he could rise again to his feet, a second thrust from Sigurd's sword had laid low the other bandit beside his comrade.

The soldier, therefore, was the only adversary that remained, and of him Sigurd thought to make short work; but in this he judged wrongly, for this robber proved to be a man of extraordinary strength and agility, while Sigurd himself was faint and jaded with his long and painful march.

For an hour that afternoon the woods resounded with the clash of swords. The two men spoke not a word, but fought with teeth set and lips closed. Once and again, by common consent, they halted, leaning on their swords for breath, but as often closed again more furiously than ever. It surprised Sigurd to find an adversary so resolute and dextrous. At another time it might have pleased him, for he loved courage even in an adversary; but now, when every hour lost meant peril to Ulf, his bosom swelled with wrath and disappointment. By force of superior weight he drove his adversary back inch by inch, till at the end of an hour the two stood some yards distant from the spot where the fight began.

Yet, though falling back, the soldier kept a bold guard, and while not inflicting any wound on his enemy, was able to ward off all blows aimed at himself.

At length, when for a moment Sigurd seemed to flag in the combat, the man gathered himself together for one mighty stroke at the hero's head. It fell like a thunderbolt but Sigurd saw it in time and caught it on his uplifted sword, and with such force that the soldier's weapon broke in two, and he himself, overbalanced by the shock, fell backwards to the ground.

Then Sigurd, with a glance of triumph, planted his foot on the body of his prostrate foe, and prepared to avenge the delay of that hour's combat.

The man neither struggled nor called for mercy, but looked boldly up in his victor's face and awaited death with a smile.

The sword of Sigurd did not descend. Some passing memory, perchance, or some soft voice breathing mercy, held it back. He drew back his foot, and sheathing his weapon, said—

"Keep thy life, and return and serve the king thy master."

The man lay for a moment as one bewildered, then springing to his feet, and casting from him his broken sword, he knelt and cried—

"Oh, merciful knight, to thee I owe my life, and it is thee I will serve to the world's end!"

"Peace!" said Sigurd, sternly; "this is no time for parley. I must be in Jockjen this night. Follow me if thou wilt thus far."

Talbot Baines Reed

And with that he began to stride once more forward with rapid steps, followed closely by his late adversary.

Sigurd uttered not a word, but walked with sword drawn as before, fearing nothing save to arrive too late at Niflheim.

Once, as they neared Jockjen, two other robbers rushed out from the woods as if to attack him, but when they perceived the stalwart champion who followed hasten forward and place himself beside the traveller, they refrained, and departed suddenly the way they came.

And now they were come at last to Jockjen. But when Sigurd made as though he would enter the town, his follower hastened to overtake him, and said—

"My knight, avoid this town, for Ulf, the king, is here, and has commanded that no stranger enter it."

"Is Ulf here?" inquired Sigurd. "They told me he was at Niflheim."

The man looked strangely at him.

"My lord," said he, "you know what only a few know. Ulf is to beat Niflheim."

"When?" demanded Sigurd.

"This night," said the man.

Sigurd answered nothing, but walked on quickly. The man, seeing that he was determined to enter the town, followed cautiously and at a distance, waiting to see what might happen.

It was evening as Sigurd entered Jockjen. The little town, overshadowed by its grim fortress, was astir with unwonted bustle. For the king's marriage on the morrow had brought together many of the country people, who, though they loved not Ulf, loved a pageant, and a holiday to see it in. And besides them many soldiers were there who talked mysteriously at street corners, and seemed to have other business than merry-making on hand.

Sigurd passed unheeded through the streets, keeping his face hid in his cloak, and avoiding all points where the crowd seemed large or curious.

He was hastening thus stealthily down a by-street which led towards Niflheim, when he suddenly became aware of a small group of men before him, under the shadow of a high wall, in eager talk.

He halted, for, by their eager gestures and cautious looks, he judged them to be desperate men, whom it would be well for him to avoid rather then meet. Withdrawing quickly into a deeper shade, he waited with impatience till their conference should be over.

As he waited he heard them speak.

"By this time," said one, "he should have learned what is in store."

"Doubtless," said another. "Yet I am glad it was no earlier, for it will all be over before he can prevent it."

"Ulf once dead," said the first, "Sigurd cannot help being the king, however much he may dislike it."

"Nay, he dislikes not being king, but he is so foolishly tender

Talbot Baines Reed

about his brother."

The other laughed.

"There are others, I trust, will not be foolishly tender with his brother this night. At what hour is the deed to be done?"

"By midnight."

At this Sigurd, who had heard it all, could not refrain from starting where he stood.

The men heard him in an instant, and finding themselves thus discovered, rushed with one accord on the hero.

Before Sigurd could draw his sword or offer any resistance he was overpowered and held fast by his assailants who, for fear he should cry aloud and alarm the town, threw a cloak over his head and led him off quickly to the castle.

Here, when the guards came out and inquired what it all meant, "This man," they said, "we know to be an enemy of the king's, who has come disguised to this town to do him some harm; keep him fast till the morning."

The guard, without so much as uncovering Sigurd's face, hurried him through the gate, and brought him to a dark dungeon, into which they thrust him, turning the key twice upon him.

Then Sigurd cast himself on the floor in despair.

To find himself thus confined, after all the fatigues he had suffered and all the perils he had escaped, was fearful indeed, the more so because he knew his brother was close at hand, and yet must die with no brotherly hand to help him.

For himself he cared nought. The men who had cast him there called themselves his friends, and, as he knew, desired only to keep him fast, believing him to be a stranger who might disclose their plot. When all was over and Ulf dead, they would release him and perchance discover who he was.

Sigurd wished he might die before the morning.

But presently, as he lay, he heard a sound of feet on the pavement without approaching his dungeon.

The door slowly opened and a monk stood before him.

The hope that dawned in Sigurd's breast as the door opened faded again as a gruff voice without said—

"Do thy work quickly, father. A short shrift is all the villain deserves."

With that the door closed again, and Sigurd and the monk were left in darkness.

"I am to die, then?" asked the hero of the holy man.

"'Tis reported," said the monk, "you seek the king's life; therefore in the morning you are to die. But," added he, speaking lower, "you shall not die, my lord."

Sigurd started, not at the words, but at the voice that uttered them.

"Who art thou?" he whispered.

"One who owes thee his life, and would repay thee, my lord. I am he whom thou sparedst but lately in the wood."

Talbot Baines Reed

In the dark Sigurd could not see his face, but he knew he spoke the truth.

"Quick," said the man, throwing off his gown and hood; "off with thy armour, my lord, and don these. There is no time to spare."

For a moment Sigurd paused, amazed at the man's offer. Then the thought of Ulf decided him.

"Brave friend," said he, "Heaven bless you for your aid. For four hours I accept thy deliverance and borrow my freedom. If before then I have not returned, call me a coward and a knave."

"Speak not of borrowing, my lord," said the man. "Heaven forbid I should require again the poor life thou thyself didst give me."

"Peace!" said Sigurd, quickly casting off his armour and covering himself in the monk's garb.

In a few moments the exchange was made. Then Sigurd, grasping the hand of his brave deliverer, pulled the hood low over his face, and stepped to the door and knocked. The guard without unlocked the door, and as he did so the robber, crouching in a distant corner of the dungeon; clanked his arms and sighed.

"Ha, ha! brave monk," said the guard to Sigurd, laughingly. "This villain likes not your news, 'tis clear. You have done your task, the headsman shall soon do his."

Sigurd said nothing, but, with head bent and hands clasped, walked slowly from the cell and on towards the gate.

Here no man stopped him, but some more devout than the rest rendered obeisance, and crossed themselves as he passed.

Once out of the castle Sigurd breathed freely, and with thankful heart quickened his pace through the fast emptying streets in the direction of Niflheim.

A double care now pressed on him. The first on account of his brother's danger, the other lest he himself, in his efforts to save the king, should be detained, and so unable to keep faith with the brave man he had left in his place in the dungeon.

He therefore pressed on with all speed, unheeded by passers-by, to whom the sight of a monk hurrying on some mission of mercy was no strange thing.

In due time, in the dim twilight, the castle of Niflheim rose before him, and he felt that his journey was nearly done.

Late as it was, there was revelling going on in the palace. Knights and ladies crowded the halls, whilst without, in the outer rooms, persons of all degrees congregated to witness the festivities and share in the hospitalities of the royal bridegroom. For though Ulf was hated by all, some, either through fear or greediness, failed not to keep up a show of loyalty and even mirth in the royal presence.

Sigurd entered the palace unchallenged, and mingled with the outer throng of onlookers. No one noticed him, but he, looking round from under his hood, could see many faces that he knew, and amongst them the conspirators whom he had that evening overheard plotting in the streets of Jockjen. The sight of these men doubled his uneasiness, for the appointed hour was nearly come, and unless he fulfilled his errand forthwith he might yet be too late.

Talbot Baines Reed

He therefore approached a knight whom he knew to be still faithful to the king, and drawing him aside, said—

"Sir, I would speak with the king. I have great news for him."

"You cannot speak to-night, holy friar," said the knight, "for the king is banqueting. Come in the morning."

"It may be too late in the morning," said Sigurd.

"Why, what news have you that is so urgent?" demanded the soldier.

"I bear news of Sigurd, the king's brother, who is approaching, and may be here to-night."

"Ha!" exclaimed the knight, eagerly; "Sigurd advancing! How many has he with him? and does he come in peace or war?"

"You know," said Sigurd, "there is no peace between Ulf and Sigurd; but I pray you take me to the king, for I have more news that will not bear delay."

At this the soldier went, and Sigurd waited anxiously.

The knight soon returned.

"The king," said he, "will see you anon, after he shall have spoken to four worthy citizens of Jockjen who have craved a secret audience."

So saying he left him and advanced to where the conspirators stood expecting to be summoned.

Then Sigurd could contain himself no longer. With hurried strides, pushing his way among the crowd, he followed and overtook the knight before he could deliver his summons. Seizing him fiercely by the arm, in a way which made the man of war start in amazement, he led him aside, and said eagerly—

"Sir, I must see the king before those men." The knight, in anger at being thus handled, cast him off roughly. But Sigurd would not be daunted.

"Bring me to the king," he said, "or I will go to him without thy leave."

The knight, amazed at being thus spoken to, looked round, and made as though he would summon the guard; but Sigurd seeing it, and now grown desperate, caught him by the neck, and putting his mouth to his ear, whispered something, which done, he drew back, and for a moment lifted the hood from his face.

The knight started in amazement, but quickly recovering his presence of mind, stepped aside with Sigurd.

Then Sigurd, knowing the man to be loyal and trustworthy, hurriedly told him all, and charged him to be secret, and see to his brother's safety.

The knight begged him to remain and see the king; but Sigurd, fearing all delay, and feeling that his task at the castle was done, would not stay, but departed forthwith.

Before he had well left the place the four conspirators were arrested, and lodged in the deepest dungeon of the fortress. The guards, especially such as stood near the person of the king, were enlarged, the guests were quietly dispersed, and that night Ulf slept secure at Niflheim, little dreaming of the peril he had escaped or of the brother who had saved him.

Sigurd, meanwhile, light at heart, sped on the wings of the wind back to Jockjen. People wondered at the wild haste of the monk as he passed. But he looked neither right nor left till he stood once more at the great gate of the castle.

The guard stood at the entrance as before.

"Thou art returned betimes, holy father," said he, "for our prisoner is like to want thee for a last shrift presently."

Great was Sigurd's joy to learn that he was in time, and that the man he had left behind lived still.

"When is he to die?" he inquired.

"Before an hour is past," said the guard.

"For what crime?"

The guard laughed. "You are a stranger in Ulf's kingdom, monk, if you think a man needs to be a criminal in order to die. But, in truth, the king knows nothing of it."

"What is the man's name?" said Sigurd.

"I know not."

"Did you see his face or hear his voice?"

"No; why should we? We could believe those who brought him here."

"And were they the king's officers?"

"The king's that is now," said the guard.

"Why?" exclaimed Sigurd; "what do you mean? Is not Ulf the king?"

"No," said the man. "When you went out two hours ago he was, but now Sigurd is king."

"False villain!" cried Sigurd, catching the fellow by the throat; "thou art a traitor like all the rest."

The soldier, astonished to be thus assailed by a monk, stood for a moment speechless; and before he could find words Sigurd had cast back the hood from his own head.

The man, who knew him at once, turned pale as ashes, and, trembling from head to foot, fell on his knees.

But Sigurd scornfully bade him rise and summon the guard, which he did. Great was the amazement of the soldiers as they assembled, to see a monk bareheaded stand with his hand on the throat of their comrade. And greater still did it become when they recognised in those stern, noble features their own Prince Sigurd.

Before they could recover their presence of mind, Sigurd held up his hand to enjoin silence, and said—

"Let two men go at once to the dungeon and bring the prisoner out."

While they were gone the group stood silent, as men half dazed, and wondered what would happen next.

In a few moments the two guards returned, bringing with them the prisoner, whom Sigurd greeted with every token of

Talbot Baines Reed

gratitude and joy.

"Brave friend," he exclaimed, "but for thy generous devotion this night might have ended in murder and ruin, and these knaves and their friends might have done their king and me a grievous wrong. Accept Sigurd's thanks."

"What!" exclaimed the prisoner, falling on his knees, "art thou Sigurd? Do I owe my poor life to the bravest of all heroes?"

"I owe my life to thee, rather," said Sigurd; "and not mine only, but my brother's." Then turning to the bewildered and shame-struck soldiers, he said—

"Men!—for I scorn to call you friends!—it remains for you to choose between your duty or the punishment reserved for traitors. You may thank Heaven your wicked plans for this night have been foiled, and that, traitors though you be, you do not stand here as murderers also. Let those who refuse to return to their allegiance stand forward."

Not a man moved.

"Then," said Sigurd, "I demand a pledge of your loyalty."

"We will prove it with our lives!" cried the men, conscience-struck, and meaning what they said.

"All I ask," said Sigurd, "is, that not a man here breathes a word of this night's doing. Besides yourselves, one man only knows of my being at Niflheim, and he has vowed secrecy. Do you do the same?"

The soldiers eagerly gave the required pledge.

"I leave you now," said Sigurd, "at the post of duty. Let him who would serve me, serve my king."

"We will! we will!" cried the men.

Sigurd held up his hand.

"It is enough," said he; "I am content. And you, friend," said he to the late prisoner, "will you accompany me home?"

The man joyfully consented, and that same night those two departed to the sea, and before morning were darting over the waves towards the Castle of the North-West Wind.

Sigurd's secret was safely kept. Ulf, to the day of his death, knew nothing of his brother's journey to Niflheim; nor could he tell the reason why the loyalty of his soldiers revived from that time forward. He died in battle not long after, yet he lived long enough to repent of his harshness towards his brother, and to desire to see him again. Messengers from him were on their way to the Tower of the North-West Wind at the time when he fell on the field of Brulform. Sigurd's first act after becoming king was to erect a monument on the spot where Ulf fell, with this simple inscription, which may be read to this day, "To my Brother."

Talbot Baines Reed

CHAPTER SIX

SUB-CHAPTER I

MY FIRST TRAGEDY

FOREWORD

I have admired tragedy from my earliest days. I believe I must have acted in it in the nursery—at least the scenes I have in my mind appeared to me to be tragic at the time, although it was not of my own will that I participated in them. The occasions, for instance, when I was stood in the corner for misconduct at table, or thrashed by my big brother for my "cheek," or dosed with castor oil by the doctor for "mulligrubs," all stand out in my memory as tragic, and no doubt prepared me to appreciate tragedy later on as a fine art.

As soon as I went to school I found still more extended opportunities for studying that art. Tragedy dogged my footsteps and marked me for her own from the first. I was bullied; that was bad enough. I was caned; that was worse. I had to learn Latin verbs; that was worst of all. I was a practised tragedian at seven. Acts one, two, and three were performed as a rule once a day, and now and then encored.

The worst of it was that the person who got most of the applause was not the wretched actor, but the author. I was quite overlooked. This convinced me early that it is more profitable to make tragedies for other people to act than to act in them oneself; and at a tender age, therefore, I set before myself the profession of a tragic author.

For long enough, however, I had to wait my inspiration. I was kept so busy in the capacity of actor (from which my special talents would not permit me to retire as early as I should myself have wished) that it was comparatively late in life—I mean I had turned twelve—before the grand idea of writing a tragedy dawned in my ardent breast. Even then it was destined to simmer for three or four years, owing to pressure of other work and the still more pressing lack of a subject.

Meanwhile, however, I read tragedies ardently. I read Shakespeare, more or less, and admired him rather, although I could see his weak points, and thought him considerably overrated. I had also read the nursery rhymes carefully, and most of the harrowing stories of history and fiction, particularly the latter. I had, moreover, recently made a tragic acquaintance with the Greek Drama in the person of a scoundrel called Aeschylus, whose sickening lucubrations I was forced to learn by heart, and now and then to copy out, a hundred lines at a time, till I grew to detest him.

All these circumstances combined decided me to write a tragedy on my own account; which, while following Shakespeare in his good points, should avoid his weaknesses, which should embody the best features of the nursery rhymes, and which should avoid like poison the shockingly debased style of Aeschylus.

After mature reflection I hit upon a theme which I flattered myself was original and suggestive. Shakespeare had kept off it, and it was after Aeschylus' time; and as far as I knew I was the first to clothe it in a tragic garb. I refer to the story of Romulus and Remus. It was classical, sanguinary, and sounded well on a title-page. Besides, as very little was known about it, there was plenty of scope for original treatment, and no one could say whether I was wrong in my facts, because no one was in a position to contradict me. In addition to that, as the story related to boys and athletic sports (both of which subjects I knew something about), it seemed the very theme of a good tragedy, which might make my name immortal, and rank to all generations as an English classic.

It might have, but somehow it didn't. However, I have kept the copy still, and this book shall be the fortunate medium of introducing the tragedy to the world.

In case any of my readers, as is possible, should be unacquainted with the story of Romulus and Remus, let me say that I believe (but am not quite sure) that they were two twin brothers, both boys, left orphans at an early age, and nursed by a stepmother in the shape of a wolf. They were subsequently discovered, and having grown to manhood, it occurred to Romulus to build Rome. For this modest undertaking Remus chaffed his brother, and practised the high jump over his walls, naturally damaging them consi- derably. Whereupon Romulus knocked him on the head, and lived happily ever afterwards.

This, briefly, is the story. Now for the tragedy:—

Romulus and Remus; Or, Catching Him On The Hop.

(The sub-title was a concession to the democratic tastes of the present generation, who like to have their curiosity excited without being told too much.)

Dramatis Persona.

Men. Romulus (a boy). Remus (his brother). John (a shepherd). Faustulus (a policeman).

Women. A Wolf. Mary Ann (a maiden of forty).

Chorus, Soldiers, Sailors, Volunteers, Bricklayers, Boys, Maidens, and Lictors.

Act I.

Scene I.—A Wood near Rome.

Enter She-wolf with two boys in her mouth, John following.

John. She-monster, tell me, what have you got there?

Wolf. Two kids, my John; and dinner-time is near.

Rom. and Rem. Oh my! alas! help! hi! Will no one hear?

John (smacking his lips). Say, gentle Lupus, where didst find them both?

Wolf. Listen! I'll tell you while you lay the cloth.

(*Sings*).

> I'm a wolf, I'm a wolf, in this big lonely wood,
> And I live in a hole in a tree,
> And I daily prowl forth in my free, hungry mood
> To look for my dinner and tea.
> I never object to the wing of a man,

Talbot Baines Reed

Or a tender young lamb gives me joy;
But what I like best is a slice off the breast,
Or the leg, or the arm, of a boy.
To-day I'm in luck, as you plainly may see
By the morsels that kick in my maw;
Fetch a knife, fork, and spoon, John, for you and for me.
Dinner's ready! Young boys taste best raw.

Rom.
Oh, impious monster, hold thy howling jaw!
And you, John, to your flocks return once more.
Forbear to talk of eating me and Remus,
You ugly, wicked, ill-conditioned schemers.

1. Here I should remark that to be strictly accurate my
tragedy should be called a tragic opera. It abounds in songs
calculated to stir familiar chords in the breasts of a popular
and juvenile audience.

2. It may here be objected that my heroes are at this time
only a few weeks old. But instances of precocious children
(especially in tragic drama) are not unheard of; and after
careful inquiry the author is not satisfied that in the present
case the young persons in question did not speak fluently.
Allowance must, of course, be made for youthful inexpe-
rience in the matter of rhymes.

Remus.
D'you hear, you cads? Shut up, and let us be.
You shall not dine off Romulus and me!

John (in alarm).
Upon my word! What if the boys are right?
Friend Lupus, thanks—I'd rather not to-night.

Wolf (scornfully).

What? Do you funk it? Well, I call that rough.

John.
Fact is, I can't help thinking they'd taste tough.

Rom. and Rem. (excitedly).
We would! we would! we're awful tough to eat;
We're only skin and bone and gristle; and no meat.
(*They sing*).
Two little kids from nurse are we,
Skinny as two kids can be;
Never a bite since yesterday,
Two little kids from nurse.

Dropped we were by our cruel ma
(With full consent of our awful pa)
Into the stream of the river Tiber -
Two little kids from nurse.

We were nearly drowned, when the stream stood still
And left us dry (and hungry) till
This old she-wolf came to take her fill
Of two little kids from nurse.
You let us be, or we'll tell our ma,
And she'll inform our awful pa;
If he comes round, you'll catch a Tartar—
Two little kids from nurse.

Wolf (turning pale).
Your words alarm me! Gentle lads, behold,
I'll be your nurse until you're two years old.
Then if you have not found your pa or ma,
I will adopt you. What say you?

Rom. and Rem..
Hurrah!

Talbot Baines Reed

John.
So now that's settled, let's chant one more strain,
And after that I'll to my home again.

Song.

Rom..
Who ran to gulp me where I lay,
And took me in her mouth away,
And talked of eating me to-day?
The she-wolf.

Rem..
Who scrunched my arm and clawed my side,
And would not heed me when I cried,
But whispered, "Won't he taste prime fried?"
The she-wolf.

John.
Who wouldn't spare two pretty boys,
Until they kicked and made a noise?
Who ever thus her time employs?
The she-wolf.

Wolf.
Who's not as bad as people say?
Who's going to nurse you night and day,
And wash your face and help you play?
The she-wolf?

(*Exeunt dancing.*)

Scene II.

The Same. Six Years Later.

Enter Romulus and Remus, fighting with boxing-gloves. The wolf knitting and looking on and encouraging.

> *Wolf.*
> Your little hands were never made
> To black each other's eyes,
> And yet you do it very well
> For youngsters of your size.
> Keep down your guard. Good! Hit out fair,
> That's one for Remus' nose!
> Ha, Romulus, you caught it there
> (Keep steady with your toes!).
> Don't lose your tempers—it's not right.

The author's motive in thus lightly treating the opening scenes of his hero's career is to postpone the gloom of the tragedy to a later period.

> Time! Let 'em blow a bit.
> My! how I like to see 'em fight!
> It sends me, in a fit.

(Has a fit and suddenly exit)

> *Rom. (discovering her absence).*
> Alas, my brother! orphans once again,
> We're left in this lone world of woe and pain.
> Our step-dame's gone, and left us no address.
> What's to be done? We're in a pretty mess.

> *Rem.*
> Let's sit and howl, and howl till some one hears.
> You do the howling, and I'll do the tears.

(They sit and howl for twenty minutes)

Talbot Baines Reed

Enter Faustulus (an old, old policeman).

Faust..
Oh dear, what can the matter be?
Romulus, Remus, *what* can the matter be?
Remus, Romulus, what *can* the matter be?
Why do you sit there and howl?
You really do make such a horrible noise,
You naughty, bad, dirty-faced blubbering boys!
Why don't you run home to your ma and your toys?
Come, clear out of this, and move on.

Rom. (screwing his knuckles into his eyes).
We 'ain't got no home and we 'ain't got no ma,
We 'ain't got no notion whose childer we are,
And our old nuss has sloped without saying "Ta ta."
Bo-ho and bo-hoo and bo-how!

Faust, (starts and drops his truncheon).
Why, these are the lost 'uns! My eyes and my stars!
Wasn't Ilia your ma's name, and your pa's name was
Mars?
There's a dollar reward for who finds you, my dears!
Hurra and hurroo and hooray!

(They all rejoice and sing.)

It will be perceived that in addressing a policeman Romulus
adopts a mode of speech which a person accustomed to deal
with the lower orders would more readily understand than
classical English.

Chorus. Oh, what a surprise!
Won't they open their eyes?
To see us two back? Oh, and won't they look black?
Oh, what a surprise!

Faust. The fact is, young gents, if you'll excuse me addressing you in prose, which I ain't a heddicated cove myself, but my gal's 'usband's uncle was a schoolmaster, only he caught cold in 'is eyes and went on the pension; very comfortable his place is in the harmsouses, which they do keep them neat and tidy enough to make one afeared to step over the door, and being long steps, 'tain't so easy for an old chap as 'as spent forty-three years come next Michaelmas in the country's service, bar six months for the dropsy and four for a broken leg, all on account of a homblibus slipping to the horf side and ketching me—

Rem. Never mind about all that. What is the fact?

Faust. Ah, I forgot. The fact is, young gents, if you'll—

Rom. Go on, go on, or we'll kick you.

Faust. The fact is, young gents, as I was saying when you threatened to kick me, you've been rather shabbily used. There's a chap of the name of Amulius. Know him?

Rom. and Rem. What, our uncle? Rather.

Faust. Well—[you'll find all about it in Smith's Classical Dictionary]—the fact is, it's 'im as done it. It's 'im as chucked yer into the river. I 'elped 'im—no, no, I don't mean that—I was passing by and see 'im at it.

Rom. (kicking him). You did? Why didn't you get us out?

Faust, (rubbing his leg). Don't do that; it hurts. Why, it was this way. When I married my old woman about forty years ago, I said to myself, says I, if ever I grow up to be a man, I shall either go into the force or else take to the sheep-farming. Oh, young gentleman, if you kick me again I shall arrest you for assault. Really I will.

Rom. and Rem.. Cut your story short. What about Amulius?

Faust. Only he's collared your crowns—that's all. Don't mention it. Take my advice and go and crack his. *Rom. and Rem.* Certainly. We'll do it at once.

(*They do it at once*)

Act II.

Scene I.

On the Banks of the Tiber. Ten Years Later.

Enter Romulus, Remus, bricklayers, maidens, and others.

Rom..,
'Tis done. The proud usurper bites the dust.
Rem.
(It's took us ten good years to do it. That's the wust.)
Rom.
The tyrant's ashes moulder on the plain.
Rem. (You've said that once before. Say it again.)
Rom. Remus, my blackguard brother, hold thy tongue.
Rem. Romulus, may I be spared to see thee hung.
Maidens.
Alas! to see two brothers bicker thus is sad,
Let's laugh and sport and turn to something glad.
Mary Ann (blushing).
I'll sing you a simple ballad if you like.
(*All shuddering*). Good gracious! (*Aside*) Certainly, by all means.
Mary Ann.
How doth each naughty little lad

Delight to snarl and bite,
And kick and scratch, It's very bad,
It isn't at all right.
Oh, don't do this; oh, don't do that,
Don't tear each other's hair,
But shout and play with ball and bat,
Or dance with maidens fair;
Play tennis, cricket, kiss-in-the-ring,
Rounders or golf or catch,
Play baseball, rounders—anything, But please don't fight
and scratch.

Run quarter miles, or hurdle race,
Jump high or low or wide;
Try football tricks, both drop and place,
Join us in seek and hide.
But *please* don't squabble, dear boys,
It isn't nice to squall;
It looks so bad, makes such a noise,
It quite upsets us all.

All.
Enough, dear Mary Ann, enough, enough;
(Did ever mortal hear such stupid stuff?)
Who's going to fight? We're here to play,
Reserve your lectures for some other day.

(*Athletic sports begin. The crowd looks on, as Chorus*)

Chorus.
Clear the course, ring the bell,
Toe the line, start them well.
Go it, cripples! on you go!
This man's gaining, that's dropped slow!
Mind the corner! keep your side!
Save your wind! Well run! well tried!

　　　　　　　Talbot Baines Reed

One more lap! Stick to it there!
Now for a spurt! He's leading clear—
No, neck-and-neck! No, leader's done!
The best man wins! Well run! well run!
Now for the jump—four feet, all clear.
Up inch by inch. Ah, very near!
Another try. What, missed again?
He's not the winning man, that's plain.
Up, four foot six! Bravo! Well jumped!
See, number four is getting pumped.
Good, number six! He's all on springs!
Another inch! The tug begins!
Up, up, and up! Three men still in -
Now only two! Which is to win? Up higher!
Ah, there's one miss more! Well jumped!
Dead heat at five-feet-four.

(*During the song Romulus and Remus run and jump.
Romulus wins the race, but the high jump is a dead heat.*)

Romulus (in a temper).
Remus is a sharper,
Remus is a cheat,
Remus collared my side,
And made it a dead heat.
I'll collar Remus' side,
Whether he likes or no;
I'll not be done by him -
At least, without a row.

Remus (derisively).
Romulus, he makes a fuss
Because he's been licked by his brother.
Let him alone, and he'll go home;
Who cares for his noise and his bother?

Chorus (reproachfully).
This is the way they always go, always go, always go,
Quarrel and kick up no end of a row,
From the time they get up in the morning.
Leave them alone and let them be, let them be, let them
be;
If they can't be civil, let us agree On this beautiful May-
day morning.

(*Exeunt dancing, leaving Romulus and Remus fighting.*)

Scene II.

On the Site of Rome.

Four Years Later.

*Enter Romulus and Remus lovingly, with their arms round
each other's necks.*

Rom.
Good old Remus, ain't I fond of you!
Oh, what a brick you are! I love you so!

Rem.
I never knew a chap I liked like Romly,
So gentle, kind, good-looking, bold and comly.

Rom.
You make me blush, my Remy; *you're* the brick,
Through thick and thin I vow to you I'll stick.

Rem.
Thank you. Suppose, to mark our vows,
We raise a monument or build a house.

Rom.
Why, while we're at it, let us build a city,
The greatest in the world! List to my ditty:
(*Sings*).

This is the town that Romulus and Remus built.

These are the walls that go round the town that Romulus and Remus built.

These are the boys that built the walls that go round the town that Romulus and Remus built.

These are the poets who sing of the boys that built the walls that go round the town that Romulus and Remus built.

These are the scholars who read the poets who sing of the boys who built the walls that go round the town that Romulus and Remus built.

These are the schoolboys who learn from the scholars who read the poets who sing of the boys who built the walls that go round the town that Romulus and Remus built.

This is the book which is read by the schoolboys who learn from the scholars who read the poets who sing of the boys who built the walls that go round the town that Romulus and Remus built.

Rem.
Bravo, Romly. Let's start work at once.
You build the walls, I'll manage the finance.

Enter Chorus of Boys derisively.

Remus and Romulus built up a wall.

Romulus and Remus, mind you don't fall.
(*Strophe*) Romulus and Remus, nice pair of
schemers,
How does your city grow?
Bricks and cabbages, sticks and rubbishes,
And mud pies all anyhow.

1. The author is not quite sure what strophe and antistrophe
mean, but they appear to come in tragically here.

2. Rubbishes is apparently the nearest rhyme to cabbages
which the chorus can lay hands on for the moment.

(*Antistrophe*)
Hee-haw, Remus can saw,
Romulus tries to make plaster.
They shall have a penny a day,
What a pity they cannot work faster!

Rom. (throwing stones).
Aroint thee! Hold your row! Shut up! Go home.
Don't interfere with men who are building Rome.

Rem. (sings).
'Mid damp clay and sandy chalk, and blue slate and loam,
Be it ever so Roman, there'll be no town like Rome.
So all do your worst, we care not who come,
There's no town like Rome, there's no town like Rome.
Rome! Rome! Great, great Rome!
There's no town like Rome, there's no town like Rome.

Chorus, disgusted.
How do these busy little lads
Delight to toil and fag,
And swagger like a pair of cads,
And boast and crow and brag.

(*Exeunt with their noses in the air.*)

Rom.
Thank goodness they are gone. Now, old chap, to work.
Sit up! you're getting lazy. Come, don't shirk.

Rem. (turning red).
I getting lazy! Like your awful cheek!
I've done more in a day than you in a week.

Rom.
Ha, ha! ho, he! My! that's a pretty joke.
Look what I've done. *You've* hardly done a stroke.

Rem.
If that's your tune, you're free to do it all.
Your work, indeed! Do you call *this* a wall?
I'd hop it on one foot. Ho, ho! A pretty town.
A puff of wind would blow your rampart down.

Rom.
Hop it, you ass? I'd like to see you try.
I promise you shall know the reason why.

Rem. (laughing).
Stupid old Romulus
Sat on a tumulus
Trying to build a town,
There came this young brother,
One foot over t'other,
And knocked his precious wall down.
Hurroo! here goes! stand clear! this for your wall!
What care I if from now to Christmas Day you bawl?
(*Hops over the wall, knocking off the top course.*)
Missed it! Hard luck! I'll try again! Stand by!
I guess I ought to clear what's barely three feet high.

Rom. (aside).
I've stood this long enough! The time has come
When I or Remus, single-handed, must build Rome.
Ho! stay thy impious foot, thou scoffing mule,
Or I will slay thee! Cease to play the fool!

Rem. (sings).
Over the city wall, over the city wall,
See how we bump, hop, skip, and jump,
Over the city wall.

(*Jumps again*)

Rom. (picking up a scaffolding-pole).
Thy doom is sealed!
I said I'd kill thee! Ha!
'Tis thy last jump! Thou hoppest never more!

(*Knocks him on the head.*)

Rem.
I've overdone it! Now I'm slain! Alas!
I do repent that I have played the ass!

(*Dies.*)

Rom. (sings).
Remus he would a-fooling go
(Heigh-ho! says Romly),
Whether his brother could stand it or no,
With a Romly, Remy, Roman, and Grecian.
(Heigh-ho! says Romulus Romly.)

Enter She-wolf suddenly.

Wolf.

Talbot Baines Reed

Hullo, my lad! I've caught you then at last!
I've waited twenty years to break my fast.
It's hungry work. But now I've got you.
Come. Don't kick, 'twill hurt the more. Fe, fi, fo, fum!

1. A classical quotation having special reference to the anticipation of a good square meal.

Rom.
Oh, please it wasn't me! See, there's my brother,
He's far more on his bones than me, my dear stepmother!

Wolf (perceiving Remits).
Humph! I may want you both.
But if you wish I'll start on Remus for my opening dish.

Rom.
Do, gentle step-dame; then when he is done,
Come back and claim your sole surviving son.

Wolf.
Agreed! But lest you should forget your promise, dear,
I'll take, if you'll allow, my first course here.
I shan't be long; and as your turn comes next,
Don't keep me waiting—I should be so vexed.

(*Proceeds to devour Remus with relish.*)

Rom. (aside).
Ah, ha, old glutton! Ha, not much you don't!

If I can help it, dine off me you won't.
(*Stabs the wolf from behind.*)

Wolf.
Alack, I die, my banquet, half untasted!

To think of so much dainty dinner wasted!

Rom. (dances and sings) -
Who killed old Remus?
I, said his brother, likewise his step-mother,
I killed old Remus.
Who saw him fall?
Not a man-jack saw him drop on his back;
None saw him fall. Who's all right now?
I, says the Roman; I'm rid of my foeman,
I'm all right now.

Enter Chorus (with a band and flags).

Great Romulus, we're glad to see you licked him
(Sing hey the jolly Roman and his ma);
We're jolly glad you punched his head and kicked him
(Sing hey the jolly Roman that you are).

Then hail to you, great Roman!
We yield to you or no man,
(Sing hey the jolly Roman and his ma).
We beg you'll let us help you build the city
(Sing hey the jolly city that he rears);
We'll be your loyal subjects; show us pity
(Sing hey the jolly city and three cheers).
Then hail the jolly city,
To you we chant our ditty,
(Sing hey the jolly city and three cheers).

Rom.
Friends, thank you one and all; excuse my tear,
Domestic trouble makes me feel so queer;
But if you like, to celebrate this day
I sing you here one final roundelay.

Talbot Baines Reed

(Sings.)
When Romulus from Tiber's stream escaped,
His infant footsteps to the woodland shaped,
He sort of vowed, if ever he grew big,
He would the walls of a great city dig.
This was his object; here he takes his stand,
Romans ever, ever, ever I'll command.

Chorus (all going)—
Rule, old Roma, Roma rule the land,
Romans ever, ever, ever he'll command.

(Exeunt omnes.)

CHAPTER SEVEN

A NIGHT WITH THE CROWNED HEADS

SUB-CHAPTER I

THE ARREST

It was a ferociously hot day at the beginning of the summer vac. I, as in duty bound, had been spending my first day as a well-conducted, newly broken-up schoolboy should.

Being fully impressed with the importance of combining self-improvement with all my recreations, I had been in the morning to the Zoo, where I had eaten buns with the elephant, cracked jokes and nuts with the monkeys, prodded the hippopotamus, got a rise out of the grizzly, made the lions roar, had a row with the chimpanzee, and generally enjoyed myself.

Then I had done the Tower. This only took ten minutes, as the place was horribly slow, and fellows looked after you wherever you went.

After that I had had a turn at the circus, to study the habits of the horse in a state of nature. I should have liked this more if

Talbot Baines Reed

the clown had not been such a muff. He wasn't half up to his business, and consequently the place was not as improving as it ought to have been. So I shook off the dust of it from my feet, and, after laying some apples and other things aboard, took an omnibus to Madame Tussaud's, where I knew I should see some fellows of my acquaintance, and be able to improve my mind in good company.

You must know I had pulled off the third history prize in our division last term, and therefore felt more or less friendly disposed to the kings and queens generally, and was even a little curious to see what they looked like, now that I was supposed to know more about them than most fellows do.

To tell the truth, although I had several times been to Madame Tussaud's before, I had invariably cut these grand people and devoted myself to another part of the establishment, which boys are usually supposed to understand better. Even on the present occasion it was necessary to pay a visit to those regions, since several celebrated historical figures were kept down there, which I felt I must on no account miss seeing.

But after I had thoroughly explored that portion, making the acquaintance of all the new-comers, putting my head into the guillotine, taking a turn in the condemned cell, sitting in Napoleon's carriage, and otherwise informing myself concerning the seamy side of human nature, I determined to be virtuous and devote at least half an hour to the study of the royalties in the Great Hall.

The enterprise was not to be undertaken without refreshment. I therefore took a preliminary excursion to the ground floor, where the historical costumes are kept, and, close beside them, the ices, buns, Victoria sandwiches, ginger-beer, Turkish delight, lemon squashes, and other wholesome aids to historical research. Here I dallied a little—just long enough to repair the ravages of nature—and then, feeling very much as Little Jack Horner did after he had partaken of refreshment, I mounted once more the marble stairs and set myself to do the crowned heads.

I set myself literally, for it occurred to me I could do their Majesties just as well sitting as standing. And, as the afternoon was hot, and the sofa near the door was comfortable, and as, moreover, I was slightly oppressed with my study of the costumes downstairs, and considerably soothed by the strains of Madame Tussaud's orchestra, it so fell out that, just as I was nodding how-do-you-do to William the Conqueror, I dropped asleep.

How long I slept I must leave it to those of my readers who have come through the same exertions of mind and body to guess. I had never intended to exceed a short forty winks, because I was aware that only half an hour was left before the time for closing arrived. But when I awoke it was with a start, to find that the place was silent, dark, and deserted. The music had gone, the shuffling of footsteps on the stairs had ceased, the hum of voices had died away. All was so quiet that my own breathing sounded loud and noisy.

I rubbed my eyes and looked round. Yes, I was on the same seat, but not a soul was left in the place—only I—I and the wax figures.

The lights were out, all except one solitary gas-jet over the door of the Chamber of Horrors, which sent a flickering gleam my way, and danced weirdly in and out among the motionless images around me. It was not a comfortable position to be in, and I confess I did not like it. Of course a wax image in the dark is the same as a wax image in the day. Still, thought I, I would sooner be outside, and—

Talbot Baines Reed

What was it made me stop short, and sit up in my seat, petrified, and with the blood curdling in my veins?

My eyes, while I meditated, had turned towards William the Conqueror, to whom, as I have already said, I had been in the act of nodding in a friendly way when I dropped asleep.

To my horror, I now perceived that he was, in a most unmistakable manner, nodding at me! Yes, by the feeble light I could see, not only his head move, but even his eyes too! I was helpless and speechless. I could no more move, or call out, or take my eyes off him, than if I had been a wax figure myself.

Presently I saw his hands move slowly to the arms of his chair, and then, keeping his eyes still on me, he rose to his feet. I could hear the clank of the sword against his greaves as he stepped off his platform on to the floor of the hall and advanced a step towards me. Then, as I sat quaking there, I felt his eyes upon mine, and knew that he was staring at me from head to toe.

By a superhuman effort I dug my fingers into the plush of the sofa, and ejaculated a frantic "Oh!"

The cry resounded fearfully through the building, and seemed to wake echoes which certainly had nothing in common with my voice. It was as if every one in the place had suddenly caught sight of me at the same moment and was giving vent to his or her astonishment.

I had better have remained silent! For, as I gave one scared look round, I saw King John lay down his pen, and, rising hastily, walk towards me. He scowled viciously at me, and then, as I collapsed in a heap on to the floor, I saw him turn inquiringly to William the Conqueror.

Whatever the question he asked was, William answered it in the affirmative, whereupon John turned round to the rest of the company, and beckoned with his hand.

Instantly William Rufus, Henry the First, Stephen, Matilda, Henry the Second, and Richard Coeur de Lion, came forward. William the Second turned me over with his foot, and stooped down to look at my face.

"That's him!" said he.

"That's he, you mean," said Henry Beauclerk.

"I mean nothing of the kind," said Rufus. "I mean him. So now, old lampreys!"

"They were *not* lampreys," said Henry sulkily; "they were oysters."

"Yes, yes," said Matilda. "But what business has *he* here?"

"Him?" said Rufus doggedly.

"You'd better ask him," said Stephen, with a sneer. "The chances are he'll want to know what business *you* have here."

"I'm as much an empress as you," said Matilda, spitefully.

"I know that; which means you're no empress at all."

"Look here," said Henry the Second, "don't you cheek me, Steevie. She let you have it pretty hot, you know."

"Hot? I like that," said Stephen. "It was cold enough that day she made tracks in the snow. I've had rheumatism ever since."

Talbot Baines Reed

"By the way," said Henry the Second, "I can put you up to a capital cure for rheumatism. Tried it myself. It was after that *little* affair about Beckett, you know. I was a good deal run down; and I got a fellow to touch me up on the shoulder with a cat. You've no notion how it picks a fellow up. Quite my own notion, too. Come, and I'll give you a dose."

"Don't mind the governor." said Richard; "he will have his joke. Did you ever read the *Talisman*, Tilly?—jolly story!— all about yours truly. You can get it for 4 pence ha'penny. I say, what's to be done with this chap, Johnny? He's a little like Arthur of Brittany, isn't he? Suppose, just to keep your hand in—"

Here John turned very red, and got into a towering rage, and threatened to tear up the Magna Charta to spite them all. Whereat they all laughed.

All this time I lay, bewildered and speechless, on the floor. It was a long time before they could bring their minds to decide what was to be done with me; and, indeed, I began half to hope they had forgotten me in their own squabbles, when a great burly form pushed his way into the group, and asked what all the noise was about.

"As if I haven't noise enough in my place with all my six wives talking at the same time," said he, "without your row. What is it? Can't you settle it and be done?"

William Rufus turned me over again with his foot.

"That thing's the matter," said he.

King Hal stooped down, with his hands on his knees, and stared at me. Then he gave a low whistle.

"Whew!" said he. "That's a catch and a half. Where did you get him?"

"Here, a quarter of an hour ago," said William the Conqueror. "It was me nobbled him."

"Not me—*I*," said Henry the First.

"You!" exclaimed the Conqueror. "Why, what do you expect if you tell lies like that?"

"I didn't mean I got him," explained Henry. "I meant you should say it was *I*."

"I shan't say it was you, when it was me," said William. "I'm not given to that style of thing, I can tell you."

"No, no," began Henry again. "What I mean is, that instead of saying it was *me*—"

"Who said it was you? I said it was me."

"Yes, and that's where you make a mistake. You should say—"

"Look here," said Henry the Eighth, "suppose you settle that outside. The thing is—whoever nobbled him, as William says—hadn't we better give him a cold chop, now we've got him?"

"Better try him first," said John. "I make a strong point of that in Magna Charta, you know."

"Much easier to take the chop first," said Henry.

"I prefer stakes myself," said Queen Mary, joining the party.

Talbot Baines Reed

"Well, well, any way you like," said King Hal; "anything for a quiet life. The ladies are worrying me to give them a day out, and an Old Bailey trial will be a nice variety for them. Only, let's have it done in proper state, if we have it at all. I suppose you'd like me to be judge, eh?"

Nobody seemed particularly pleased at this proposal; and Richard said—

"You'd better ask Elizabeth, hadn't you?"

"Oh, good gracious, no!" exclaimed Henry in alarm. "Don't say a word about it to her, or there'll be a terrible rumpus. I assure you I have studied law all my life. Come along. Bring him downstairs and let's begin. Here, Teddy," cried he to a nice-looking boy not far off, who must have been Edward the Fifth. "Here, Teddy, run and tell Catherine, and Annie, and Janie, and Annie Cleeves, and Kitty Howard, and Kitty Parr—let's see, is that all?" said he, counting them over on his fingers; "yes, six—tell 'em all to hurry up, and not to let Elizabeth see them, whatever they do. Oh, and you can tell all the lot of Majesties after Johnny here they'd better come, too. Come, look alive, my lad."

"All, very well," said Teddy; "how am I to look alive after the way I've been served? Besides, I can never remember all their names."

"Well, look them up in the catalogue—they're all down there. Tell them, the big dock downstairs. And if we're lucky and get the job over in time, I don't mind standing treat all round in the refreshment-room afterwards. That will fetch them, I fancy; eh, what?"

SUB-CHAPTER II

THE TRIAL

The room suddenly grew dim and silent again, and I began to think that after all I had been only dreaming. But when I lifted my head and looked round, the place of the kings was empty. There was William the Conqueror's footstool where he had upset it; and there lay the pen and ink on the floor under King John's chair. As for the big group in the middle, not a soul was left there except Chaucer and William Caxton, who had taken possession of the two easiest chairs, and were deep in a game of chess.

As I picked myself slowly up off the floor, I became aware of the gleam of a lantern approaching me, and heard a footstep coming down the hall. It was too dark to see who it was till he was close up; then, with a gasp, I recognised Marwood, the hangman!

"Oh," said he pleasantly, "you're the young party, are you? Come, cheer up. You've got to be tried first. The fact is, they couldn't find the regular police, and asked me to step up for you. Come, my lad," said he, proceeding to pinion me with the cord in his hand, "this will brace you up wonderfully. You may depend on me to do the job neatly. I've just invented a new noose, and have been wanting a light weight to try it on, so you're in luck. Come along, and don't keep them waiting."

And he proceeded to conduct me to the Chamber of Horrors. As we passed along the hall, one or two of the figures nodded to us; and Oliver Cromwell requested in Marwood to let him know when his part of the business was going to begin, as he should like to be present.

"I don't care about the trial, you know," said he. "Seen plenty of that sort of thing. But I'd like to see how you do your job, you know; so don't forget." And he slipped a shilling into Marwood's hand.

"You've no idea of the civility I receive from some of these gentlemen," said the latter to me with emotion. "Little drops of kindness like this always touch me. You shall have a little drop too, my boy, presently."

I tried feebly to laugh at the joke; but I couldn't, whereupon he got very sulky, and bundled me down the stairs without another word.

By the dim light of a few candles placed about the room I could see that the Chamber of Horrors was packed by a dense crowd of sightseers, who occupied seats on the floor of the court, and sat impatiently whispering together, expecting my arrival.

As I stumbled up the steps of the Old Bailey dock (where room had been made for me between Burke and Hare) the usual thrill of sensation passed round the court. I could see Henry the Eighth and his wives opposite me in the small dock, while the other crowned heads jostled one another on the platform of the guillotine. There, too, was the old hermit peeping out through the bars of his cage, and the warder in charge of the condemned cell was sweeping his place out and changing the sheets on the bed.

"Now then," said Henry the Eighth, when all the bustle had subsided, "wire in, somebody! Let's begin."

"You'd better get a jury first," said King John. "That's one of the first things I insist upon in Magna Charta."

"Order in the court!" cried Henry, "and Magna Charta be bothered! I shall do as I like!"

"Do have a jury, love," said Catherine Parr; "it's *such* fun when they come in with their verdict!"

"Oh, all right; have it your own way. I should have thought, though, I could come in with a verdict as well as they. Now then, you there!" said he, addressing the convicts round me, "answer to your names."

And he proceeded to call the names out from the catalogue.

When a dozen had answered, Anne of Cleeves said, "That's enough, Henry dear; we've got twelve."

"Oh, have we?" said he. "You can have more if you like, you know; there's plenty left."

The ladies, however, decided that a dozen was enough, and the trial began.

"Prisoner at the bar," said Edward the Black Prince, who was acting as usher, "are you guilty or not guilty?"

"What's the use of asking him that," said Henry the Eighth, "when everybody knows, eh?"

John here began to explain that he had arranged the matter in Magna Charta, whereupon the judge exclaimed—

"Oh, gracious! if we're to have that up every two minutes I'll adjourn the court! Now, you there!" said he to me; "why don't you answer?"

I tried in dumb show to explain that I was not aware what I

Talbot Baines Reed

was being tried for; but as no one saw the point of my answer, I tremblingly pleaded "Not guilty."

"Oh," said Henry, growing very red in the face, "all right! Now, somebody, let's have the indictment!"

To my horror, I suddenly saw reflected on a screen, in large characters, at the far end of the room, my recent examination paper, with all my answers appended thereto! As I staggered back in terror, Henry laughed.

"Too late now," said he; "you've said 'Not guilty', so you've got to be tried—got to be tried. Eh, what? Now start away; begin at the top. What's that he says about Alfred the Great? Where is Alf, by the way?"

"Oh," said Edward the Third, "he can't come. The fact is, they've taken him and dressed him up as a French General, and he's so awfully busy, he says, you'd better let his part of the thing slide."

"All serene!" replied Henry. "Lucky job for you, prisoner. I know what a rage he'd be in over that toast-and-muffin story you've been telling about him. He'd have done you brown, my boy, I can promise you! Never mind. Now let's go on to the next. Read it out, Nigger."

Edward the Black Prince, who answered to this genial pet name, accordingly read—

"'William the Conqueror was a cruel tyrant. He made many homes desolate, and wrote Doomsday Book in the year 1087.'"

"There!" cried the Conqueror, coming to the rail of the guillotine and striking it in a passion with his gauntlet; "what do you think of that? *I* wrote Doomsday Book! It's a lie. My lords and gentlemen of the jury, I can stand anything else, but when he says I wrote Doomsday Book, I say it's a lie, and I hope to see him hung!"

"Hanged," suggested Henry the First.

"All right, all right," said Henry the Eighth, "keep cool, and you shall see him hung, and Henry shall see him hanged. We'll oblige all parties. So you mean to say, Willie, you never did such a thing?"

"No, never; I hope I know my place better," said the Conqueror; "and I'm surprised at you for asking such a question."

"Got that all down, Nigger?" asked the judge.

"Yes. Forge ahead!" said the Black Prince. "Now we come to the next, 'William the Second, surnamed Rufus, shot in the New Forest, by Walter Tyrrell.'"

"Eh?" shouted Rufus, pushing his father aside, and coming to the front. "What's that? Me shot by Walter? Me—"

"Do say *I*," suggested Henry the First.

The Red King rounded on him at once.

"Oh!" he cried, "it was you, then, was it? You're the one that did it! I guessed as much! I knew you were at the bottom of it all along. What do you think of that, my lords and gentlemen?"

"The thing is," drawled Edward the Second, "did Walter—"

"Order in the court!" cried Henry the Eighth. "Kindly allow me to conduct my own case. All you've got to say, Rufus, is whether it's true what he says, that Walter Tyrrell shot you?"

"Him!" cried Rufus. "He couldn't hit a haystack a yard off, if he tried."

"Then he didn't do it? That's all right. Why couldn't you have said so at once? All down, Nigger? That makes two lies. Now call up the next."

"Henry the First, surnamed Beauclerk, never smiled again after his son was lost, and died of a surfeit of lampreys," read the prince.

"Oh, those lampreys!" groaned Henry; "I am perfectly sick of them. I assure you, my lords and gentlemen, they were no more lampreys—"

"No, not after you'd done supper," growled Rufus.

"In that case, William," retorted Beauclerk, "I should have said 'there,' and not 'they.' But I do assure you, gentlemen, I never saw a lamprey in my life; and as for smiling again," added he, in quite an apologetic way, "I did it often, when nobody was by; *really I did.*"

"Are you sure?" asked the judge. "Show us how you did it."

Whereupon Henry the First favoured the court with a fascinating leer, which left no doubt on any one's mind that he had been falsely accused.

So two more lies were set down against me; and the Black Prince called over the next.

"'Stephen usurped the throne on Henry's death.'"

"Quite right, quite right," said Matilda; "perfectly correct."

"'Matilda, after a civil war, in which her bad temper made her many enemies—'"

"Oh you story!" exclaimed the empress. "Oh! you wicked young man!"

"Address the judge, please," said Henry the Eighth.

"Oh, you wicked young man," repeated the empress, turning to the bench; "I'd like to scratch you, I would!"

"Don't do that," said Henry: "I get quite enough of that at home, I assure you. Anyhow, Nigger can chalk it down a lie for you, eh?"

"And one for me, too, please," said Stephen. "How can a fellow usurp what belongs to him?"

"Give it up," said Coeur de Lion. "Ask another."

"Silence in the court," cried the judge. "Put it down, Nigger, and for mercy sake drive on, or we shall be here all night."

"'Henry the Second murdered Thomas a Becket, and was served right by having a family of bad sons,'" read the usher.

"That's nice!" said Henry, advancing. "Bad sons, indeed! Never had a better lot in all my life. Really, my lord, that ought to count for four lies right off. The idea of calling my Johnny a bad boy. Why, my lord, he was his father's own boy. You've only to look at him; and if he was a bit of a romp, why, so were you and I in our day."

"Speak for yourself," said Henry the Eighth severely. "But what about Becket?"

"Ah, well, there was a little accident, I believe, about him, and he got hurt. But I assure you I never touched him; in fact, I was a hundred miles away at the time. I'll prove an alibi if you like."

"No, no," said the judge; "that is quite sufficient. Chalk down two, Nigger: one for Becket and one for the bad family. How many does that come to?"

"That's eight," said the Black Prince. "All right. We only want two more. Go on."

"'Richard the First, surnamed the Lion Heart, was the strongest and bravest man in England, and won many glorious battles in the Holy Land.'"

"Hullo, I say," said the judge. "That's pitching it just a little strong, isn't it? What have you got to say to that, Dicky?"

"Seems pretty square," said Richard modestly. "He doesn't say what a good dentist I was, though. My! the dozens I used to pull out; and—oh, I say—look here, he says nothing about Blondel, and the tune I composed. That's far more important than the Crusades. It was an andante in F minor, you know, and—"

"That'll do, that'll do, Dicky. We've heard that before," interrupted the judge. "Score him down half a lie, Nigger, and call up Johnny."

"'King John, surnamed Lackland, was a wicked king. He was forced to yield to the barons, and he lost all his clothes in the Wash.'"

"Well, I never!" said John, foaming with rage; "if that isn't the coolest bit of lying I ever heard! Here have I been and worn my fingers to the bone writing Magna Charta and giving England all her liberties, and he never once mentions it! My lord and gentlemen, I should like to read you the document I hold in my hand, in order that you may judge—"

"What, eh? Read that thing?" exclaimed Henry the Eighth, in horror. "You'd better try it on, that's all. Good gracious me, what next? I've a good mind to commit you for contempt of court. The question is, were you a wicked king? and did you lose your clothes in the Wash?"

"I am surprised and pained that your lordship should ask me either question. When I assure you, my lord and gentlemen, that a more dutiful son, a wiser monarch, a tenderer husband, and a more estimable man than the humble individual who now addresses you, never drew—"

"Teeth," put in Richard I.

"No, breath," continued John. "And when I further tell you that I never even sent my clothes to the wash, and therefore could not possibly have lost them there, you will—"

"All right, pull up," said the judge. "That'll do. Keep the rest, my boy. That makes ten and a half—more than we want. Now, then, the next thing is, what sort of execution shall we have?"

"Oh, please," said the ladies, "*please*, Harry, darling, let the jury go out and bring the verdict in. It will be such fun."

"Eh, what?" said Henry, "oh, bother the jury! Where are they? Clear out, do you hear!" said he, addressing the twelve. "Go up to the Napoleon room and talk it over, and stay till I send for you."

The jury obeyed, and I was left alone in the dock.

"Now," said the judge, evidently relieved, "let's have the execution."

"But we've not had the verdict yet," said Anne Boleyn.

"That'll do any time," said Henry. "Just as much fun to have it afterwards. Besides, it's a wonderful saving of time to get the execution over now, while we're waiting; and then we can go straight to the refreshment-room. Eh, girls? Eh, what? Ah, I thought so."

"Oh, well," said Catherine of Aragon, "but *do* put him in the condemned cell for a minute or so, and then have him brought out, like they all are, and—"

"*As* they all are," said Henry the First. "Like is only used when—"

"Hold your tongue, you impertinent, forward young man!" said Catherine in a rage. "There, now!" added she, beginning to cry, "I've forgotten what I was going to say, all through you!"

"I think," said Henry the Eighth, waving his hand for silence, "he'd better be hung. Marwood tells me it's a very pretty sight; and the gallows are there quite handy. Besides," added he confidentially, "we should have to tip him in any case, so we may as well let him have the job, and get what we can for our money. What, eh?"

Every one approved of this, and the executioner was summoned.

Then, as I stood there, shivering in every limb, unable to speak, or even to move, I was aware once more of the lantern coming towards me, and of a hand laid heavily on my shoulder.

"Come, young gentleman," said the voice, "wake up—or you'll get locked in. They're shutting the doors. Tumble up, and look sharp."

It was Madame Tussaud's porter; and I had been fast asleep, after all!

Talbot Baines Reed

CHAPTER EIGHT

A STORY OF THE CIVIL WARS

SUB-CHAPTER I

THE INTERRUPTED FEAST

The Singletons were a small Lowland clan, or rather faction, for their name does not appear in history as a clan. For all that, they were as loyal to their king and as devoted to their chief as any clan in Scotland, and when the time for sacrifice and hard blows came, the Singletons, as every one knew, were ever to the front.

And it is only fair to say the Singletons were *always* in the wars. When they were not fighting the Roundheads they were fighting the Campbells or the Frasers or the Macintoshes, or others of their hereditary foes; or if none of these were obliging enough, or at liberty to indulge them in their favourite pastime, then they made enemies for themselves among the neighbouring clans, or else crossed over to Holland to keep their hands in there till fortune favoured them once more at home. The old castle, with its rambling towers, and walls, and buttresses was a sort of rallying-point for all the pugnacious spirits of the time, and its bluff walls showed many a scar and many a dint where hostile guns had played upon them, not, you may be sure, without reply.

The Singletons, in fact (and specially since the old laird had died), thrived on fighting. At the present day they might, perhaps, have passed as freebooters and outlaws, but during the troubled times of the Commonwealth they were looked upon as a noble band of patriots, whose swords were ever ready in the king's cause, and whose castle was as open and hospitable to a friend as it was unyielding to a foe.

Such was the place within whose weather-beaten and war-beaten walls a festive company was assembled one November afternoon in the year of our Lord 16—.

For once in a way the Singletons were at peace. The king's cause was for a time under a cloud, and the Campbells and the Frasers and the Macintoshes were far too busy about their own affairs to come out of the way to defy this small bulldog of a clan in the south. The Singletons had serious thoughts of invading some place, or sacking some castle, or making a raid across the border, just to pass the time. It was like being out of work! They fretted and chafed in their fortress, and nearly fell out among themselves, and very heartily wished some one would give them a pretext for a fight. But no one did.

It was at least a diversion for them to celebrate the coming of age of the young laird, and the event, which in times of war might have passed scarcely heeded, now became one of mighty importance to these restless Singletons.

They called together every man of the name who could easily be found between the Solway and the Tay. They hoisted the old family ensign on the castle walls, and by way of mischief some of them displayed the pennant of the

Macfies—another rival clan—below it. They drove in twelve head of oxen, regardless of proprietorship, wherewith to make good cheer at table, and they decked the grand old banqueting-hall with branches and heather, till it was more like a bower than a room.

These and many other things the Singletons did by way of showing honour to the occasion, and when that evening thirty of them sat round the festive board, with the young chief at the head, and with pyramids of beef and mutton and bread before them, their satisfaction and enthusiasm reached its highest pitch.

"Here's luck to the Singleton!" shouted they, "root and branch, laird and clan."

And amid cheers, prolonged and deafening, the health was honoured and the banquet proceeded.

"Was ever luck like ours?" growled one youth to his neighbour. "Here have we been six weeks idle, with never a knock."

"And it'll be six weeks longer before we get one again, I'm thinking, unless the king's party gather," said his comrade. "We don't get our fair share of fighting, Tam, that's what it is."

"May be the young laird will change all that. But, I say, Donald, I have my doubts of it."

"What, of the young laird?" exclaimed the others.

"Ay, he's been brought up in a queer school in England, they tell me, where it's considered ill-breeding to molest your neighbour."

"Do you say so? The barbarians! That would never do for us, Tam. But of course the young laird taught them better?"

"They say they taught him worse, and that—Well, never mind. What is auld Geordie saying?"

Auld Geordie was on his feet, announcing with great glee that a convoy of treasure, bound for Edinburgh, was on its way at that moment from Newcastle, so he had heard, and would pass within three miles of Singleton Towers.

"And it'll be ours, boys," cried the old man, turning to his comrades; "and the young laird shall win his spurs upon it! What do you say?"

A shout was the only answer. The proposal was one after the Singletons' own heart. Every one looked towards the young laird.

Singleton was a dark, mild-looking youth, old for his years, and up till the present time a stranger to his clan. For, as has already been hinted, he had but just returned from England, where his boyhood had been spent, to celebrate his coming of age. Great things were expected of him, not only as the head of the clan, but as the son of his brave father, who had died twelve years ago; and since whose death the Singletons had been leaderless. With a bold leader they might achieve anything; and they now welcomed the presence of a chief once more in their midst with all the hope and confidence of sons welcoming a father. It was, therefore, with astonishment and dismay that they heard him reply to auld Geordie's proposal—

"I did not know the Singletons were highwaymen!"

If the roof had fallen in it could not have caused greater

consternation. The Singletons looked aghast to hear such a speech from their chief!

"Is the boy mad?" said one in a whisper.

"Or a coward?" said another.

"Or a fool?" said another.

"The laird's joking," said auld Geordie, in a coaxing voice; "and we are glad to see ye so merry. But ye'll be in earnest to-morrow, I warrant, with a score of troopers between you and a thousand pounds!"

"I'm in earnest now," replied young Singleton. "I'm no robber chief, I tell you. The convoy shall go safe to Edinburgh, as far as we are concerned. But, come now, Geordie, I want to hear something about this old castle of mine, for you know I was scarcely in it since I was a boy."

But it was easier to turn the talk than to turn the thoughts of his clansmen. They experienced, all of them, a distinct disappointment at this first exercise of authority on the part of their young laird; and the cheeks of some of the younger among them actually coloured with shame at the thought that a Singleton—the Singleton—should be lacking (as they could not help thinking he was) in bravery. However, they said nothing, but seemed to listen to auld Geordie, as he launched out into an account of the old castle of Singleton Towers.

"It's a brave old place," said he. "Sir David Singleton it was who built it here, on this arm of the sea, in the time of King Wallace. The story goes that Wallace himself set the top stone of the great tower with his own hands. Sir David did not live long to enjoy the stronghold, as you have heard."

"How did he die? I never heard that," asked the young laird.

"Alas! it is a sad story, though a short one. Sir David had a son, and that son was a coward—the first, and we hope the last, coward who ever bore the name."

Here all looked hard at the youth, who, not noticing their meaning glances, said—

"Amen, with all my heart! Go on."

"Well, this son grew up, like you, in England, and it was not till he had reached man's estate that he came here. His father, a proud man, and ambitious, rejoiced, as your father would have rejoiced this day, to see a son in his place, ready, as he hoped, to carry on the brave traditions of his name to a future generation. The youth was welcomed home with great pomp and rejoicing, and for aught men could see he was a worthy son of a worthy sire.

"But, alas! as the Bible says, 'Pride comes before the fall.' A few days after his home-coming, the news came that a party of English was advancing on Singleton Towers. The old laird, nothing doubting, ordered his son to take fifty men and meet the enemy, while he himself stayed behind to guard this place.

"The lad obeyed, and marched forth. They met, he and the English, under Brantor Hill yonder; and then appeared the real character of the boy. At the first onset, before ever a blow was struck, he turned and fled, no one knows whither.

"The old laird for long would not believe it; but when on all hands the story was confirmed, and no news came of the lad, he sickened and drooped. He shut himself up in the turret-room out there and never left it except at night, when his one

Talbot Baines Reed

walk was on the east terrace, over this very room.

"One night they missed the sound of his footsteps, and next morning he was found dead in his little chamber—dead of a broken heart. And they say that if ever again a coward should be the laird of Singleton, that that old man will walk out there where he walked four centuries ago."

A dead silence followed the close of this story, and all eyes, by a sort of common instinct, were turned towards the head of the table. At that moment, apparently from the terrace outside, came a sound of footsteps; and as they listened, every cheek grew suddenly pale, and a shudder crept round the assembly. The silence, however, was broken by a laugh from the young laird himself, who had been the only unmoved hearer of this last mysterious sound.

"Why, there is my poor dog, Jupiter, out there! I had quite forgotten him. Let him in, some one!"

No one stirred. The young chief looked round perplexed, and then rose himself and went to the window and opened it. As he did so, a huge shaggy mastiff bounded into the apartment, barking and capering for glee at seeing once again his master and hearing his voice.

"Lie down, sir, quiet. Now, my men, what think you of this for a ghost? Thanks, Geordie, for your story. I remember now, I heard it when a child. Well, let's hope it will be a long while yet before Sir David's ghost is put to the trouble of a midnight walk."

"Hist, my young master," said Tam; "it's ill jesting with the spirits."

"What, Tam! one would think, now, by the way you speak,

you would not dare to keep a solitary watch on the east terrace yourself."

"I'd dare anything," replied Tam, "but—"

"But you would rather not," replied Singleton, laughing.

That laugh roused the spirit of Tam, who, though superstitious, was hardly a coward.

"I never said that," he cried; "and if needs be I would do it, even to- night."

"*Even* to-night!" repeated Singleton. "What does the man mean? *Even* to-night! I've a good mind to order you to the watch to-night for talking in riddles, sirrah!"

"The watch here has always been a double one since I can remember," put in auld Geordie.

"To my mind, one man ought to be able to watch as well as two, for the matter of that. And so, Tam, you mean you would be more comfortable with a comrade on the east terrace to-night. Perhaps Sir David would oblige you," he added, with a laugh.

The soldier flushed angrily.

"Ay, you may say that," he muttered, in an undertone; "it's more than likely Sir David *will* be walking to-night."

The boy caught these last words, and glanced quickly at the speaker. The meaning of these mysterious utterances suddenly flashed upon him. These men, then mistook him, their chief, their captain, for a coward!

A crimson flush suffused his face, a flush of shame and anger, as he sprang to his feet.

At that instant, and before he could utter a word, a bugle sounded at the gate, and there entered the hall a soldier whose appearance bore every mark of desperate haste.

"Singleton," he cried, as he entered, "the king's friends are up! Glencairn musters his men at daybreak at Scotsboro', and expects the thirty men of the Singletons promised him, there and then!"

Here was a piece of news! The long-wished-for summons had come at last, and the heart of each Singleton present beat high at the prospect of battle! And yet in the midst of their elation a serious difficulty presented itself.

"Thirty men!" said Geordie, looking round him. "Why there are but thirty-one men here, counting the laird. Some must stay."

But the young laird, who had noticed the same thing, cried out promptly to the messenger—

"Tell your general he shall have his thirty men before dawn," and with that the soldier withdrew.

The joy of the Singletons now gave place to something like panic, as they comprehended what the rash pledge of their young chief really meant. It meant that thirty of them must go, and one must stay; and what could one man do to defend a castle like Singleton Towers? The elder soldiers were specially concerned.

"Call him back, Singleton," said Geordie. "You cannot leave this place defenceless! Think of the peril! Ten men must stay, at the least."

"Who says 'must' to me?" cried the young chief, impatiently. "Are the Singletons to be word-breakers as well as highwaymen? Thirty men shall go. Have we not promised?"

"But who will stay?" asked some one.

"Ah, that's it," cried another. "Who is to stay?"

Silence ensued on the question, and then—

"*I* will stay," quietly replied Singleton.

"You! The laird!" shouted every one, in amazement. "That can never be!"

"Why not?" inquired the youth. "Who is chief here, you or I?"

"But who is to lead us in battle?"

"Ah," said Singleton, "that is my duty, I know, but it is equally my duty to stay here!"

"But it is certain peril, and you could do no good. Let one of us stay. Let me stay with you," said Geordie.

"No, brave Geordie, you must go. It must never be said the Singletons broke their word, even to save their castle. Take the thirty men to Glencairn. If he permits ten to return, well and good. You will find me here."

"But your place is at our head," said the men.

"And there I will be to-morrow. To-night I watch here; ay, and on the east terrace with Sir David, Tam," he added, with a smile. "But come; to horse there! You lose time. Bring out the guns! On with your belts, men! Be brisk now! Take every man some bread and meat from the table!"

And with these words the martial fire of the father blazed out in the son, so that his men wondered more than ever how they could have suspected him of faint-heartedness.

"Are you all equipped and mounted? Lower the drawbridge there! Open the gate! Forward, men! and 'Singleton for the king!'"

And waving his hand he bade them march forth, and watched them slowly defile across the drawbridge and turn their horses' heads eastward.

The last man to cross was Tam.

"Heaven protect you," he said, humbly, "and forgive me for the insult I put upon you." Then reining in his horse, he added, almost beseechingly, "Once again, let me stay with you."

"Not I," replied young Singleton, gaily. "Forward, Tam, and to-morrow, if you return, you shall hear how I fared."

Tam said nothing, but setting spurs to his horse, bounded across the drawbridge and rejoined his comrades.

Singleton, having watched the troop as they slowly wended their way among the trees of the wood till they were lost to sight, drew up the bridge and closed and barred the great gate. Then, with a stout though anxious heart, he turned and addressed himself to his solitary and hazardous undertaking.

SUB-CHAPTER II

THE NIGHT WATCH

The young laird of Singleton turned slowly from the courtyard out of which his men had just ridden, back into the castle.

Young as he was, and inexperienced, he knew enough of the state of his country to feel that the task which he had imposed upon himself was one of the greatest peril, not only to his own life, but to the ancestral castle of his clan, for the country swarmed with freebooters and hostile clans, on the look-out for any chance of plunder; and they, if only they got wind of the unprotected state of Singleton Towers, would lose no time, he knew, in striking a blow during the absence of the clan, which might end in the loss of the old fortress for ever. Still, what else could he have done? He was bound in honour to fulfil his pledge to the royal cause by sending the thirty men, and as for himself, he had no hesitation in deciding that, for this night at least, the post of duty, if not of honour, was on the ramparts of his own castle, even though on that account the Singletons must ride leaderless to the king's standard.

Besides, it must be confessed, there was a spice of adventure about the undertaking which well accorded with his bold spirit; and as his thoughts went back to the scene of the banquet and the suspicions entertained there as to his own courage, it pleased him to reflect that, whatever happened, a Singleton would never again be able to charge his chief with cowardice.

It was nine o'clock and quite dark when he turned from the gateway out of which his men had just sallied, and retraced his steps slowly into the deserted castle. His solitary foot-steps sounded weird and lonely across the paved yard which a few minutes before had rung with the clatter of horses and the bustle of preparation. Still more solitary did they sound as he passed on his way through the deserted passages, and found himself once more in the old banqueting-hall, where the feast remained still on the board, and the empty chairs all round, just as the clansmen had left them to obey the sudden and urgent order to march forth.

But dreariest of all did they sound as, forcing open a small and long disused door, which grated back on its hinges and groaned as he did so, he stepped out on to the east terrace.

Before he did this, however, he took all the wise precautions necessary to insure, as far as possible, the safety of the old castle, and in some respects this was not a difficult task, for Singleton Towers stood at the head of a narrow arm of the sea, which on three sides completely surrounded it, leaving only the east side assailable by land.

On the sides of the sea the castle rose perpendicularly from the water, the only entrance being by way of a creek, half cave, half boathouse, the entrance to which could at pleasure be barred by a portcullis. This precaution Singleton took, and had the satisfaction of feeling that on its seaboard at least the castle was as secure as if a garrison of a hundred men watched it.

On the land side, however, security was not so possible. The water was continued in the form of a ditch twelve yards wide round this side also; but it was a narrow protection at the best. The drawbridge which spanned it was, as we have already seen, drawn up; and the great iron gate connecting with the outside world, carefully barred and bolted. Still, as Singleton looked down, he felt concerned to think how easily a few bold men could swim the moat and assault the place. But he was in for it now!

As auld Geordie had said, the guns of the castle were all loaded and ready for action; and Singleton was relieved to see that one of these was mounted on the turret over the great gate; and a further discovery relieved him still more, and that was that the woods on this side were so dense that, except along the narrow clearing through the trees, it would hardly be possible for any number of troops, especially if they brought artillery, to approach.

He therefore took advantage of the moonlight to point the gun carefully so as exactly to cover the entrance to this narrow path, a precaution which, as will be seen, stood him in good stead before the night was out.

As to the other guns, there was one on the east terrace, rusty and old- fashioned, but happily loaded; and there were others at various corners and buttresses, all of which the young laird inspected and ascertained to be ready for any emergency. He also placed muskets in readiness at various points in case of need.

All these preparations occupied a long time in effecting, and it was not till an hour had passed since the departure of his men that Singleton felt able to take his place on the watch, and quietly await the result of his venture.

He had scarcely done so, however, when it occurred to him that though all the garrison had left the place, there was still plenty of armour in the castle which might be used to good purpose. Why not set out helmets on the ramparts, and pikes as well as guns? It was a good idea. He hurried to the armoury, and quickly took from their places all the steel helmets and pikes and plumes on which he could lay his

Talbot Baines Reed

hands. These he artfully disposed on various parts of the battlements, so that to any one below it would appear that instead of one man, twenty armed warriors guarded the place.

"Who knows but these numskulls may serve me in good stead?" said the youth to himself, laughing to think what excellent substitutes for a living man an empty helmet with a spear-head beside it may be made to appear. This little artifice being satisfactorily accomplished, and lights set burning in various rooms of the castle still further to aid the delusion, he returned once more to the east terrace and began his solitary vigil.

The moon was up, and peeped occasionally from behind the drifting clouds to light up the dark scene below. As Singleton peered down from his lofty post, he could see the water sparkling below him, and catch the distant lights here and there on wood and mountain. Not a sound was to be heard but the moaning of the wind among the turrets and the distant splash of the water against the south base of the castle. Not a moving creature was to be seen, except the uneasy bats which flapped round now and then over his head. Everything below was motionless and silent, without one token of life, except, indeed, the distant light of a beacon, which tinged the sky with a lurid glare, and added a weird feature to the dark, solitary landscape.

Singleton, after a turn or two, was conscious of a half-dismal sensation and a feeling of loneliness, which, as long as he had been busily occupied, had not oppressed him. He paced quickly to and fro, whistling to himself, and determined not to yield to the effects of his position. He wondered how far his men were on their way by this time. Was old Geordie riding at their head? Suppose they were attacked, how would they come out of it? He wondered, too, if Tam was—

What was that?

A low groan from one corner of the terrace, and the clanking of a chain! Singleton halted dead, and for a moment his heart was in his mouth. Then he broke into a laugh.

"Jupiter again! That's the second time he has played ghost to-night! Well, old doggie, you've woke up, have you, and you're going to keep me company, eh?"

And then, as he resumed his march, he talked in a low voice to the dog, who rose quietly from his corner, and with soft, stealthy tread proceeded to accompany his master to and fro along the terrace.

Singleton was ashamed of himself for being as startled as he had been at this incident.

"A pretty hero I shall make at this rate," said he; "if this is the worst alarm I am to have to-night I shall get off easily, eh?"

Jupiter solemnly wagged his tail, and evidently considering he had done enough in accompanying his master some twenty turns up and down, retired quietly to his old corner, and once again composed himself to slumber.

Singleton walked on, halting now and then to make a careful scrutiny all round, and continuing to whistle softly to himself all the time.

Somehow his mind continually found itself reverting to Geordie's story. It was an old wife's tale, of course, but a queer one too. And this was the very terrace on which the old warrior used to walk, and that little turret-chamber there was his room! Ah! strange how the reflection of the moon should make it appear as if there were a light in the room! If he were not certain no light was there, he could have vowed that was one. Bah! he wished Geordie had kept his story to himself, it made him feel quite dismal.

Hark! A footstep!

He was certain he heard one, close at his side too. He stood still and listened. Everything was silent. He moved on again. There! he heard it distinctly! almost in step with his own. He looked up and down, everywhere; and then Geordie's words rushed back on his memory, "If ever again a coward should be laird of Singleton, that old man—"

Here he stepped forward, and again suddenly halted. The footstep that time was as distinct as his own. Pooh! what if it was? He was not going to be afraid of all the ghosts in Scotland! and he laughed out loud by way of assuring himself of his nerve. But he had hardly done so, when just above him sounded another laugh, mocking his own, and as he stepped suddenly forward, the footsteps began again as clear as ever.

This was more than Singleton had bargained for; and he sat down on the end of the gun in bewilderment and alarm. Had any one been there to see his face it would have appeared a good deal paler than was its wont; and it was certainly something more than the cold that made him shiver. He sat perfectly still and listened. There was not a sound. He strained his eyes on every hand. Nothing was visible through the darkness but the silent terrace on which he watched. What could it be? As he sat and wondered, the pike which had been resting carelessly across his knee slipped and fell on to the stone pavement with a sudden clank, which was instantly repeated overhead, just as the laugh and the footsteps had been.

Of course it flashed upon Singleton then—an echo! nothing but a simple echo among the nooks and crannies of the castle; and at a simple echo his cheek had turned pale and his heart had stood still, and his hands had actually trembled! He scorned himself bitterly for his cowardice; and once more, relieved in mind and humbled in spirit, set out on his night watch, determined this time that nothing, not even a score of ghosts, should terrify him.

And now the night began to wear on. By this time the men must be very near their rendezvous, for it was an hour past midnight, and the moon was getting down towards the west. He wondered what other clans would muster round the royal standard, and how soon the king's forces would be likely to meet the enemy. This time to-morrow he would be with his men; that is, provided the general permitted ten of them to return and relieve guard here. Supposing no one came!

At that moment Jupiter gave a very low growl, which made his master stop short in his march and listen with all his ears. For a long time not a sound was audible, and then he fancied he could just detect the tramp of a horse or horses in the far far distance. But that seemed to die away, and again all was utterly silent.

But once more, just as he was starting again on his walk, Jupiter growled, and this time rose to his feet and came to his master's side. Yes, it was the sound of horses somewhere; more than one, too. With straining ears and beating heart, the youth leant on his pike, and listened. The sound grew more and more distinct, and presently he could tell that, whoever they were, they were galloping. He ordered Jupiter to lie down and be silent. They were in the wood, somewhere. Were they bound for Singleton? Presently he was able to distinguish voices, and a minute afterwards it seemed as if every sound had ceased.

He stepped quietly, followed by Jupiter, from the east terrace to the rampart over the great gate, where he was able to command as full a view as the uncertain light would allow of the glade through the frees which led to the castle. But nothing could be seen. As he watched, the sounds commenced again, and this time he fancied he could detect a rumbling noise as of a cart accompanying the horsemen.

It was now easy to tell the meaning of all these sounds. A troop of horsemen—he could not yet guess how many—were approaching Singleton Towers; and bringing with them a gun!

The young laird's heart beat now in right earnest, but not with fear. That had been left behind with the ghosts. He forgot everything but the defence of his castle and the glory of his clan; and waited eagerly for the time of action.

The cavalcade made a halt about halfway through the wood, and in the still night air, with the light breeze carrying it, Singleton could hear the sound of voices as in hurried consultation. Then a single horseman approached; and before many minutes he could just discern in the dim moonlight a form emerging from the wood and stealthily approaching the castle.

"Let him come and spy," said Singleton, to himself.

"He will see the lights, and perhaps a few spear-heads on the walls—and he'll report as much to his chief. Ah!"

At that moment the clouds cleared away from the moon and clearly revealed the intruder. He was one of the Macfies, Singleton could see, and fully armed. He dismounted at the border of the wood, and advanced cautiously on foot to the edge of the moat. This he made no attempt to cross, but made his observations from the far side.

Singleton, taking care not to be seen, crept back into the armoury, from which he took a bugle. Bringing it out into the terrace, he sounded a few shrill notes; and then instantly seizing a lantern, ran hurriedly to and fro with it on various parts of the battlements. Then without waiting a moment he took up a musket and fired it in the direction of the scout, who, however, was by this time out of reach.

"There!" said Singleton, putting down his weapon; "that will satisfy them we are on the alert, all of us, and ready for them! Perhaps they will think better of it, and turn tail."

No! in a few minutes the sound of the advancing troop again rose in the night. They came on at a trot, dragging their gun along with them. Presently there was a gleam among the trees, and next moment some fifty horsemen appeared in view, with a cannon in their midst, which, equally to Singleton's satisfaction and surprise, they proceeded to get into position at the very entrance to the wood.

It was on this spot, it will be remembered, that the young laird had carefully levelled the gun that surmounted the great gate. Everything depended now on the skill with which he had aimed it. He gave the foe a minute or two to fix and point their weapon, and once more carefully calculated the poise of his own. Then, just as they were proceeding to load, and the horsemen were preparing to follow up the attack on the gate, he applied the match, and with a mighty roar the piece discharged.

It was an anxious moment while the smoke slowly cleared away. When it did he had the joy of beholding the enemy's gun on end and disabled, and not only it, but at least three of the enemy themselves involved in the same disaster.

He could not resist a triumphant cheer at this success, which was promptly answered by a defiant shout from the enraged Macfies as they set spurs to their horses and rushed towards the moat.

And now began the hard work of the night. For the foe thought nothing of such a narrow obstacle as a simple ditch. Some swam it on horseback, and some left their animals behind, but all—all except two whom Singleton's trusty muskets had found out—crossed in safety. The raid they made on the great gate was something terrific, and Singleton's heart trembled within him as he heard it creak before their united weight. But he worked away steadily at his post, always taking care not to expose himself, yet never wasting a shot with a bad aim.

The enemy very soon quitted the gate, and took to the more formidable work of attempting to scale the walls. And here Singleton's power was tried to the utmost. For at one part the ground sloped a considerable distance up one of the buttresses, which made the ascent from below comparatively easy, and if only the Macfies had been suitably equipped for an assault, they could not have failed to carry the place with ease.

But happily for Singleton, they had come very ill prepared, evidently expecting to walk into a defenceless stronghold without a blow—and now they were not only disappointed but disconcerted.

Yet there was no keeping them down eventually. In vain Singleton plied his weapon with deadly effect; in vain he dislodged and hurled down upon them one of the massive coping stones of the east terrace. As fast as the foremost fell back dead or wounded, others swarmed up. It was well for Singleton no attempt was made on any other part but this assailable buttress, and even this was scaled at last.

The young laird had stepped back hurriedly to load his weapon, when he suddenly saw a head appear above the battlements; and next moment a fierce Lowlander sprang on to the terrace.

With the butt end of his weapon Singleton felled him, while at the same moment Jupiter flew at the throat of the man next to him who was also springing on to the wall.

It was a narrow escape indeed; and but for the dog, the castle might after all have been lost. Once more the youth cleared the buttress, and this time with such deadly effect, that the enemy halted a moment before resuming the attack. This short breathing space was unutterably valuable to Singleton, for it gave him time not only to load several muskets, but to bring one of the smaller cannon in position so as to almost cover the weak point.

This precaution, however, as it turned out, was not requisite; for just as the enemy were returning with redoubled fierceness and determination to the attack, there was a shout from the wood, and a cry of "Singleton to the rescue!"

Well did the young chief know that cry. He was saved! In another moment the Macfies had too much to do to defend themselves from the sudden attack in the rear to think of renewing the assault, and the youth knew well enough how to make good use of the interval. With a loud cheer to his gallant clansmen, he kept up a dropping fire on the enemy with musket and gun, until galled on both sides, they fairly took to their heels and plunged once more into the moat.

How many came out of it and escaped, history does not record; but they left of their number under the walls of

Singleton Towers twenty men dead or wounded.

It was a proud moment when the young laird flung open the great gate and let his comrades in. The leader of the party was Tam, who had implored the general of the king's forces, whom fortunately they had met on the way to the rendezvous, to be allowed to return, if only for a few hours, to share his young laird's peril. The request had been granted, and with fifteen men the delighted Tam had spurred back to Singleton as fast as their horses could carry them. Falling unexpectedly on the enemy's rear they had brought about the panic which saved the castle and rescued the young chief from his perilous position.

This was the first but by no means the last fight in which the young laird of Singleton bore a part. He grew old in warfare, and ended his days at last on the field of battle. But to the day of his death this memorable Night-Watch on Singleton Towers was ever the achievement about which he liked best to be reminded.

CHAPTER NINE

RUN TO EARTH

SUB-CHAPTER I

ON THE TRAIL

Michael McCrane had bolted!

There was not a shadow of a doubt about it. The moment I reached the bank that eventful morning and saw the manager's desk open, and the tin cash-box lying empty on the floor, I said at once to myself, "This is McCrane's doing."

And as I and the messenger stood there, with dropped jaws, gaping at the dismal scene, I hurriedly called up in my mind the incidents of the past week, and, reading them in the light of this discovery, I was ready to stake my reputation as a paying cashier that my fellow-clerk was a robber and a fugitive.

McCrane had not been at our bank long; he had come to us from one of the country branches, and, much to the disgust of some of us juniors, had been placed over our heads as second paying cashier. I was third paying cashier, and from the moment I set eyes on my new colleague and superior I felt that mischief was in the wind.

A mysterious, silent man of twenty-six was Michael McCrane; so silent was he, indeed, that were it not for an occasional "How will you take it?"

"Not endorsed."

"Next desk," ejaculated in the course of his daily duties, any one might have supposed him dumb. He held himself gloomily aloof from his fellow- clerks. None of us knew where he lived, or how he lived. It was an event to get a word out of him; wherever it was possible he answered by signs or grimaces. He glided into his place in the morning like a ghost, and like a ghost he glided out at night and vanished.

More than that, his personal appearance was unsatisfactory. He was slovenly in figure and habits, with a stubbly beard and unkempt hair; and although he had L150 a year his clothes were threadbare and shabby. He seemed always hard up for money. He did not go out, as most of us did, in the middle of the day to get lunch, but fortified himself with bread and cheese, which he brought in his pocket, and partook of mysteriously behind the lid of his desk.

Now and then I had come upon him while he was deeply engaged in writing what appeared to be private letters, and I could not help noticing that on each occasion when thus interrupted he coloured up guiltily and hid his letter hastily away in his blotting-paper. And once or twice lately mysterious parcels had been handed to him over the counter, which he had received with a conscious air, hiding them away in his desk and carrying them home under his coat at night.

I did not at all like these oddities, and, holding the position I did, I had often debated with myself whether it was not my duty to take the manager or head cashier into my confidence on the subject. And yet there had never till now occurred anything definite to take hold of, nor was it till this October morning, when I saw the manager's desk broken and the empty cash-box on the floor, that it came over me that McCrane was even a worse fellow than I had taken him for.

He had been most mysterious about his holidays this year. He was to have taken them in May, among the first batch, but suddenly altered his arrangements, giving no reason, and requesting to be allowed to go in September. September came, and still he clung to his desk. Finally another change was announced: McCrane would start for his fortnight's holiday on the second Thursday of October.

These changes were all arranged so mysteriously, and with such an unusual show of eagerness on McCrane's part, and as the time itself drew near he exhibited such a mixture of self-satisfaction, concealment, and uneasiness, that no one could fail to observe it. Add to this that during the last day or two he had made more than one mistake in his addition, and had once received a reprimand from the manager for inattention, at which he vaguely smiled—and you will hardly wonder that my first words on that eventful morning—the first of his long-expected holiday—were—

"Michael McCrane has bolted!"

The manager when he arrived took the same view as I did.

"I don't like this, Samuels," said he; "not at all, Samuels."

When Mr Trong called any one by his name twice in one sentence it was a certain sign that he meant what he said.

"How much was there in the box?" I inquired.

"L23 5 shillings 6 pence," said the manager, referring to his petty cash account. "There was one five-pound note, but I do not know the number; the rest was cash."

The messenger was called in and deposed that Mr McCrane had stayed the previous evening half an hour after every one else, to wind up, as he said. The witness stated that he heard him counting over some money, and that when he left he had put out the gas in the office and given him—the deponent—the key of his—the suspect's—own desk.

"Bring his book," said the manager.

I did so, and we examined it together. The last page had not been added up, and two of the lines had not been filled out with the amounts in the money column. Oddly enough, when the two cancelled cheques were looked at they were found to amount to L21.

"We must go thoroughly into this," said the manager. "It looks worse and worse. What's this?"

It was a torn piece of paper between two of the leaves of the book, part of a memorandum in McCrane's handwriting. It read thus:

[A scrap of paper is illustrated here.]

"What do you make of that?" asked the manager. A light dawned on me.

"I wonder if it means Euston, 1:30? Perhaps he's going by that train."

The manager looked at me, then at the clock, and then went to his desk and took up a Bradshaw.

"1:30 is the train for Rugby, Lancaster, Fleetwood. Samuels!"

"Sir," said I.

"You had better take a cab to Euston, you have just time. If he is there stop him, or else follow him, and bring him back. If necessary, get the police to help you, but if you can bring him back without, so much the better. I'm afraid the L23 is not all; it may turn out to be a big robbery when we go through his book. I must trust to your judgment. Take some money with you, L20, in case of emergency. Be quick or you will be late. Telegraph to me how you succeed."

It was a word and a blow. A quarter of an hour later my hansom dashed into the yard at Euston just as the warning bell for the 1:30 train was sounding.

"Where for, sir?" asked a porter. "Any luggage?"

I did not know where I was for, and I had no luggage.

I rushed on to the platform and looked anxiously up and down. It was a scene of confusion. Groups of non-travellers round the carriage doors were beginning to say a last good-bye to their friends inside. Porters were hurling their last truck-loads of luggage into the vans; the guard was a quarter of the way down the train looking at the tickets; the news-paper boys were flitting about shouting noisily and inarticulately; and the usual crowd of "just-in-times" were rushing headlong out of the booking-office and hurling themselves at the crowded train.

Talbot Baines Reed

I was at a loss what to do. It was impossible to say who was there and who was not. McCrane might be there or he might not. What was the use of my—

"Step inside if you're going," shouted a guard.

I saw a porter near the booking-office door advance towards the bell.

At the same moment I saw, or fancied I saw, at the window of a third- class carriage a certain pale face appear momentarily, and, with an anxious glance up at the clock, vanish again inside.

"Wait a second," I cried to the guard, "till I get a ticket."

"Not time now," I heard him say, as I dashed into the booking-office.

The clerk was shutting the window.

"Third single—anywhere—Fleetwood!" I shouted, flinging down a couple of sovereigns.

I was vaguely aware of seizing the ticket, of hearing some one call after me something about "change," of a whistle, the waving of a flag, and a shout, "Stand away from the train." Next moment I was sprawling on all fours on the knees of a carriage full of passengers; and before I had time to look up the 1:30 train was outside Euston station.

It took me some time to recover from the perturbation of the start, and still longer to overcome the bad impression which my entry had made on my fellow-passengers.

Indeed I was made distinctly uncomfortable by the attitude

which two, at any rate, of these persons took up. One was a young man of the type which I usually connect with detectives. The other was a rollicking commercial traveller.

"You managed to do it, then?" said the latter to me when finally I had shaken myself together and found a seat.

"Yes, just," said I.

The other man looked hard at me from behind a newspaper.

"Best to cut your sort of job fine," continued the commercial, knowingly. "Awkward to meet a friend just when you're starting, wouldn't it?" with a wink that he evidently meant to be funny.

I coloured up violently, and was aware that the other man had his eye on me. I was being taken for a runaway!

"Worth my while to keep chummy with you," said the heartless man of the road. "Start a little flush, don't you?"

I ignored this pointed inquiry.

"Not bank-notes, I hope—because they've an unkind way of stopping them. Not but what you might get rid of one or two if you make haste. But they're ugly things to track a chap out by, you know. Why, I knew a young fellow, much your age and build, borrowed a whole sheaf of 'em and went up north, and made up his mind he'd have a high old time. He did slip through a fiver; but—would you believe it?—the next he tried on, they were down on him like shooting stars, and he's another two years to do on the mill before he can come another trip by the 1:30. They all fancy this train."

This style of talk, much as it amused my fellow-passengers

and interested the man in the corner, made me feel in a most painful position. My looks and blushes, I am aware, were most compromising; and my condition generally, without luggage, without rug, without even a newspaper, enveloped me in such an atmosphere of mystery and suspicion that I half began to wonder whether I was not an absconding forger myself.

Fortunately the train stopped at Willesden and I took advantage of the halt to change my carriage, explaining clumsily that I should prefer a carriage where I could sit with my face to the engine, whereat every one smiled except myself and the man in the corner.

I tried hard to find an empty carriage; but the train was full and there was no such luxury to be had. Besides, guards, porters, and station-masters were all shouting to me to get inside somewhere, and a score of heads attracted by the commotion appeared at the windows and added to my discomfort. Finally I took refuge in a carriage which seemed less crowded than the rest—having but two occupants.

Alas! to my horror and dismay I discovered when the train had started that I had intruded myself on a palpably honeymoon couple, who glared at me in such an unfriendly manner that for the next hour and a half, without respite, I was constrained to stand with my head out of the window. Even in the tunnels I had no encouragement to turn my head round.

This was bad enough, but it would have been worse had it not happened that, in craning my head and neck out of the window, I caught sight, in the corner of the carriage—next to mine, of half of the back of a head which I felt sure I knew. It belonged, in fact, to Michael McCrane, and a partial turn of his face left no doubt on the matter. I had run my man down already! I smiled to myself as I contemplated the unconscious nape of that neck and recalled the gibes of the commercial traveller and the uncomfortable stare of the man in the corner.

What should I do? The train would stop for two minutes at Bletchley, and not again until we reached Rugby. Should I lay my hand on his shoulder at the first place or the second?

I wished I could have dared to retire into my carriage and consult my timetable about trains back. But the consciousness of the honeymoon glare at my back glued me to the window. I must inquire at Bletchley and act accordingly.

We were beginning to put on the break, and show other signs of coming to a halt, when I was startled by seeing McCrane stand up and put his head out of the window. I withdrew as hastily as I could; not daring, of course, to retreat fully into the carriage, but turning my face in an opposite direction, so as to conceal my identity. I could not guess whether he had seen me or not, it had all occurred so quickly. If he had, I might have need of all my strategy to run him to earth.

As the train pulled up I saw him lower his window, and, with anxious face, make a sudden bolt across the platform.

That was enough for me. I darted out too, much to the satisfaction of my fellow-travellers.

"When's the next train back to Euston?"

"Take your seats!" bawled the guard, ignoring me.

"When does the next train go to Euston?"

"There's a time-table there."

I went; keeping one eye on the train, another on the spot where my man had vanished, and feeling a decided inconvenience from the lack of a third with which to consult the complicated document before me. In a rash moment I ventured to concentrate my whole attention on the timetable. I had found Bletchley; and my finger, painfully tracing down one of the long columns, was coming very near to the required latitude, when I became aware of a whistle; of a figure, bun in hand, darting from the refreshment-room to a carriage; of a loud puff from the engine.

I abandoned the time-table, and rushed in the same direction. Alas! the train was in full motion; a porter was standing forbiddingly between me and my carriage, and the honeymoon couple were blandly drawing down the blinds in my very face! Worst of all, I saw the half-profile of Michael McCrane, inflated with currant bun, vanish; and as the end carriage whirled past me I received a friendly cheer from the commercial traveller, and a particularly uncomfortable smile from his silent companion in the corner.

I was left behind! The bird had flown out of my very hand; and there was nothing now but to return in confusion and report my misfortunes at the bank.

Stay! I could telegraph to detain my man at Rugby. Let me see. "To Station Master, Rugby. Detain Michael McCrane— bank robbery—tall, dark—third-class—left Euston 1:30—I follow—Samuels." How would that do? I was pleased with the look of it; and, in the fullness of my heart, consulted the station-master.

He eyed me unfavourably.

"Who are you?" he had the boldness to inquire.

"I'm from the bank."

"Oh!" he said; and added, "your best plan is to follow him in the supplemental. It will be up in five minutes. He's sure to be bound for Fleetwood, and you'll catch him on the steamer. They won't stop him on the road without a warrant. They don't know you."

I admitted the truth of this, and, after some inward debate—particularly as I had a ticket through—I decided to take advice, and avail myself of the "Supplemental."

It was painfully supplemental, that train—a string of the most ramshackle carriages the line could muster, and the carriage in which I found myself smelt as if it had been in Billingsgate for a month. However, I could sit down this time. There was neither honeymoon, commercial traveller, nor man in the corner to disturb my peace; only a rollicking crowd of Irish harvest men on their way home, in spirits which were not all of air.

I was claimed as one of their noble fraternity before we were many stages on the road; and although I am happy to say I was not compelled to take part in their potations, for the simple reason that they had none left to offer me, I was constrained to sing songs, shout shouts, abjure allegiance to the Union Jack, and utter aspirations for the long life of Charlie Parnell and Father Mickey (I believe that was the reverend gentleman's name), and otherwise abase myself, for the sake of peace, and to prevent my head making acquaintance with the shillalahs of the company. I got a little tired of it after a few hours' incessant bawling, and was rather glad, by the assistance of a few half-crowns (which I fervently trusted the manager would allow me to charge to his account), to escape their company at Preston, and seek the shelter of a more secluded compartment for the rest of the way.

I found one occupied by two files of soldiers in charge of a couple of deserters, and in this genial company performed the remainder of the journey in what would have been something like comfort but for the ominous gusts of wind and rain which, as we neared the coast, buffeted the carriage window, and promised a particularly ugly night for any one contemplating a sea voyage.

SUB-CHAPTER II

BOWLED OUT

When we reached Fleetwood it was blowing (so I heard some one say) "half a cap." I privately wondered what a whole cap must be like; for it was all I could do, by leaning hard up against the wind, and holding on my hat—a chimney-pot hat, by the way—to tack up the platform and fetch round for the Belfast steamer, which lay snorting and plunging alongside.

It takes a very good sailor to be cheerful under such circumstances. I felt profoundly melancholy and wished myself safe at home in my bed. The sight of the black and red funnel swaying to and fro raised qualms in me which, although still on *terra firma*, almost called for the intervention of a friendly steward. Alas! friend there was none.

In my desperation I was tempted basely to compromise with duty. How did I know Michael McCrane was on the steamer at all? He might have dropped out at any one of a dozen wayside stations between Bletchley and here. Indeed the probability was that he had. Or—and I felt almost affectionately towards him as the thought crossed my mind—even if he had come so far, he, like myself, might be a bad sailor, and prefer to spend the night on this side of the angry Channel. I could have forgiven him much, I felt, had I been sure of that.

In any case, I asked myself earnestly, was I justified in running my employers into the further expense of a return ticket to Belfast without being reasonably sure that I was on the right track? And *was* I reasonably sure? Was I even—

On the steerage deck of the steamer below me, with a portmanteau in one hand and a brand-new hat-box and a rug in the other, a figure staggered towards the companion ladder and disappeared below. That figure, even to my unwilling eyes, was naught else but a tragic answer to my own question.

Michael McCrane was on board, and going below!

A last lingering hope remained.

"Hardly put off to-night, will you?" said I to a mate beside me, with the best assumption of swagger at my command.

He was encasing himself in tarpaulins, and appeared not to hear me.

I repeated my inquiry, and added, in the feeble hope that he might contradict me, "Doesn't look like quieting down."

"No," said he, looking up at the sky; "there'll be a goodish bit more of it before we're over. All aboard there?"

"No," I shouted, rushing towards the gangway; "I'm not!"

Oh, how I wished I could have found myself just left behind. As it was I was precipitated nearly head first down the gangway, amid the by no means friendly expletives of the sailors, and landed at the bottom a clear second after my hat, and two seconds, at least in advance of my umbrella. Before I had recovered all my component parts the *Royal Duke* was off.

It was not the slightest comfort to me to reflect that if only I had dashed on board the moment I saw my man, and arrested him there and then, we might both be standing at this moment comparatively happy on that quay whose lights blinked unkindly, now above us, now below, now one side, now the other, as we rolled out of the harbour.

"Bit of a sea outside, I guess," said a voice at my side.

Outside! Then what was going on now did not count! I clapped my hat down on my head and made for the cabin door.

It had entered my mind to penetrate into the steerage at once and make sure of my runaway; but when I contemplated the distance of deck between where I now stood and where I had seen him disappear; and when, moreover, as the boat's head quitted the lee of the breakwater a big billow from the open leapt up at her and washed her from stem to stern, something within me urged me to go below at once, and postpone business till the morning.

I have only the vaguest recollection of the ghastly hours which ensued. I have a wandering idea of a feeble altercation with a steward on hearing that all the berths were occupied and that he had nowhere to put me. Then I imagine I must have lain on the saloon floor or the cabin stairs; at least, the frequency with which I was trodden upon was suggestive of my resting-place being a public thoroughfare.

But the treading under foot was not quite so bad as being called upon to show my ticket later on. That was a distinctly fiendish episode, and I did not recover from it all the night. More horrible still, a few brutes, lost to all sense of humanity, attempted to have supper in the saloon, within a foot or two of where I lay. Mercifully, their evil machinations failed, for nothing could stay on the table.

Oh, the horrors of that night! Who can say at what angles I

Talbot Baines Reed

did not incline? Now, as we swooped up a wave I stood on my head, next moment I shivered and shuddered in mid-air. Then with a wild plunge I found myself feet downward, and as I sunk my heart and all that appertained to it seemed to remain where they had been. Now I was rolling obliquely down the cabin on to the top of wretches as miserable as myself. Now I was rolling back, and they pouring on to the top of me. The one thought in my mind was—which way are we going next? and mixed up with it occasionally came the aspiration—would it were to the bottom! Above it all was the incessant thunder of the waves on the decks above and the wild wheezing of the engines as they met the shrieking wind.

But I will not dwell on the scene. Once during the night I thought of Michael McCrane, and hoped he was even as I was at that moment. If he was, no dog was ever in such a plight!

At last the early dawn struggled through the deadlights.

"At last," I groaned, "we shall soon be in the Lough!"

"Where are we?" said a plaintive voice from the midst of the heap which for the last few hours had regularly rolled on the top of me whenever we lurched to larboard.

"Off the Isle of Man," was the reply. "Shouldn't wonder if we get a bit of a sea going past, too."

Off the Isle of Man! Only half way, and a bit of a sea expected as we went past!

I closed my eyes, and wished our bank might break before morning! Whether the "bit of sea" came up to expectations or not I know not. I was in no condition to criticise even my own movements. I believe that as time went on I became gradually amalgamated with the larger roiling heap of fellow-sufferers on the floor, and during the last hour or so of our misery rolled in concert with them. But I should be sorry to state positively that it was so.

All I know is that about a hundred years after we had passed the Isle of Man I became suddenly awake to the consciousness that something tremendous had happened. Had we struck in mid-ocean? had the masts above us gone by the board? were we sinking? or what?

On careful reflection I decided we were doing neither, and that the cause of my agitation was that the last wave but one had gone past the ship without breaking over her. And out of the next dozen waves we scrambled over I counted at least five which let us off in a similar manner!

Oh, the rapture of the discovery! I closed my eyes again lest by any chance it should turn out to be a dream.

The next thing I was conscious of was a rough hand on my shoulder and a voice shouting, "Now then, mister, wake up; all ashore except you. Can't stay on board all day!"

I rubbed my eyes and bounded to my feet.

The *Royal Duke* was at a standstill in calm water, and the luggage- crane was busy at work overhead.

"Are we there?" I gasped.

"All except you," said the sailor.

"How long have we been in?"

Talbot Baines Reed

"Best part of an hour. Got any luggage, mister?"

An hour! Then I had missed my man once more! Was ever luck like mine?

I gathered up my crumpled hat and umbrella, and staggered out of that awful cabin.

"Look here," said I to the sailor, "did you see the passengers go ashore?"

"I saw the steerage passengers go," said he; "and a nice-looking lot they was."

"There was one of the steerage passengers I wanted particularly to see. Did you see one with a portmanteau and hat-box?"

"Plenty of 'em," was the reply.

"Yes; but his was quite a new hat-box; you couldn't mistake it," said I.

"Maybe I saw him. There was one young fellow—"

"Dark?"

"Yes; dark."

"And tall?"

"Yes; tall enough."

"Dismal-looking?"

"They were all that."

"Did you see which way he went?"

"No; but I heard him ask the mate the way to the Northern Counties Railway; so I guess he's for the Derry line."

It was a sorry clue; but the only one. I was scarcely awake; and, after my night of tragedy, was hardly in a position to resume the hue and cry. Yet anything was preferable to going back to sea.

So I took a car for the Northern Counties station. For a wonder I was in time for the train, which, I was told, was due to start in an hour's time.

I spent that hour first of all in washing, then in breakfasting, finally in telegraphing to my manager—

"Fancy tracked him here rough crossing—will wire again shortly."

Then having satisfied myself that none of the steamer passengers could possibly have caught an earlier train, and determined not to lose the train this time, I took a ticket for Londonderry, and ensconced myself a good quarter of an hour before the appointed hour in a corner of a carriage commanding a good view of the booking-office door.

As the minutes sped by, and no sign of my man, I began to grow nervous. After all he might be staying in Belfast, or, having got wind of my pursuit, might be escaping in some other direction. It was not a comfortable reflection, not did it add to my comfort that among the passengers who crowded into my carriage, and helped to keep out my view of the booking-office door, was the gloomy, detective-looking individual whose demeanour had so disconcerted me during the first stage of this disastrous journey.

Talbot Baines Reed

He eyed me as suspiciously as ever from behind his everlasting newspaper, and under his scrutiny I hardly dared persevere in my own look-out. I made a pretext of buying a newspaper in order to keep near the door. To my dismay the whistle suddenly sounded as I was counting my change, and the train began to move off. At the same moment a figure, carrying in one hand a portmanteau and in the other a hat-box, rushed frantically into the station, and made a blind clash at the very door where I stood. I shrunk back in a panic to my distant corner, with my heart literally in my mouth. There was a brief struggle on the doorstep; the hat-box flew in, and the door was actually opened to admit the owner, when a couple of porters laid violent hands upon him and dragged him off the train.

It was not I who had been left behind this time, but Michael McCrane; and while he and his portmanteau remained disconsolate in Belfast, I and his hat-box were being whirled in the direction of Londonderry in the company of a person who, whatever he may have thought of McCrane, without doubt considered me a fugitive!

It was a trying position, and I was as much at sea as I had been during the agitated hours of the terrible night, I tried to appear calm, and took refuge behind my newspaper in order to collect my ideas and interpose a screen between myself and the critical stare of my fellow- passenger. Alas! it was avoiding Scylla only to fall into Charybdis. The first words which met my eyes were:—

"Bank Robbery in London.—

"A robbery was perpetrated in—'s bank on Wednesday night, under circumstances which point to one of the cashiers as the culprit. The manager's box, containing a considerable amount of loose cash, was found broken open, and it is supposed the thief has also made away with a considerable sum in notes and securities. The cashier in question has disappeared and is supposed to have absconded to the north. He is dark complexioned, pale, mysterious in his manners, and aged 26. When last seen wore a tall hat, gloves, and a grey office suit."

Instinctively I pulled off my gloves and deposited my hat in the rack overhead, and tried to appear engrossed in another portion of the paper. But I could not refrain from darting a look at my fellow-traveller. To my horror I perceived that the paper he was reading was the same as the one I had; and that the page between which and myself his eyes were uncomfortably oscillating was the very page on which the fatal paragraph appeared.

I was dark, *I* was pale (after my voyage), and who should say my manners were not mysterious?

In imagination I stood already in the box of the Old Bailey and heard myself sentenced to the treadmill, and was unable to offer the slightest explanation in palliation of my mysterious conduct.

In such agreeable reveries I passed the first hour of the journey; when, to my unfeigned relief, on reaching Antrim my fellow-traveller quitted the carriage. No doubt his object was a sinister one, and when I saw him speak to the constable at the station, I had no doubt in my own mind that my liberty was not worth five minutes' purchase. But even so, anything seemed better than his basilisk eye in the corner of the carriage.

I hastily prepared my defence and resolved on a dignified refusal to criminate myself under any provocation. What were they doing? To my horror, the "detective," the

Talbot Baines Reed

constable, the guard, and the station- master all advanced on my carriage.

"In there?" said the official.

My late fellow-traveller nodded. The station-master opened the door and entered the carriage. I was in the act of opening my lips to say—

"I surrender myself—there is no occasion for violence," when the station-master laid his hand on the hat-box.

"It's labelled to C—," he said; "take it along, guard, and put it out there. He's sure to come on by the next train. Right away there!"

Next moment we were off. What did it all mean? I was not under arrest! Nobody had noticed me; but McCrane's hat-box had engaged the attention of four public officials.

"Free and easy way of doing things on this line," said an Englishman in the carriage; "quite the regular thing for a man and his luggage to go by different trains. Always turns up right in the end. Are you going to Derry, sir?" he added addressing me.

"No," said I, hastily. "I'm getting out at the next station."

"What—at—" and he pronounced the name something like "Tobacco."

"Yes," I said, pining for liberty, no matter the name it was called by.

At the next station I got out. It was a little wayside place without even a village that I could see to justify its claim to a station at all. Nobody else got out; and as soon as the train had gone, I was left to explain my presence to what appeared to be the entire population of the district, to wit, a station-master, a porter, and a constable who carried a carbine. I invented some frivolous excuse; asked if there wasn't a famous waterfall somewhere near; and on being told that the locality boasted of no such attraction, feigned to be dismayed; and was forced to resign myself to wait three hours for the next train.

It was at least a good thing to be in solitude for a short time to collect my scattered wits. McCrane was bound for C—, and would probably come in the *next* train, which, by the way, was the last. That was all I had a clear idea about. There was a telegraph office at the station, and I thought I might as well report progress to my manager.

"On the trail. Expect news from C—. Wire me there, post-office, if necessary."

The station-master (who, as usual, was postmaster too) received this message from my hands, and the remainder of the population—I mean the porter and the constable—who were with him at the time read it over his shoulder. They all three looked hard at me, and the station-master said "Tenpence!" in a tone which made my blood curdle. I was doomed to be suspected wherever I went! What did they take me for now?

I decided to take a walk and inspect the country round. It annoyed me to find that the constable with his carbine thought well to take a walk too, and keep me well in view.

I tried to dodge him, but he was too smart for me; and when finally to avoid him I took shelter in a wayside inn, he seated himself on the bench outside and smoked till I was ready to

Talbot Baines Reed

come out.

I discovered a few more inhabitants, but it added nothing to my comfort. They, too, stared at me and followed me about, until finally I ran back to the station and cried out in my heart for the four o'clock train.

About five o'clock it strolled up. I got in anywhere, without even troubling to look for Michael McCrane. If he should appear at C—, well and good, I would arrest him; if not, I would go home. For the present, at least, I would dismiss him from my mind and try to sleep.

I did try, but that was all. We passed station after station. Some we halted at, as it appeared, by accident; some we went past, and then, on second thoughts, pulled up and backed into. At last, as we ran through one of these places I fancied I detected in the gloaming the name C—painted up.

"Is that C—?" I asked of a fellow-traveller.

"It is so! You should have gone in the back of the train if you wanted to stop there."

Missed again! I grew desperate. The train was crawling along at a foot's pace; my fellow-traveller was not a formidable one. I opened the door and jumped out on to the line.

I was uninjured, and C—was not a mile away. If I ran I might still be there to meet the back of the train and Michael McCrane.

But as I began to run a grating sound behind me warned me that the train had suddenly pulled up, and a shout proclaimed that I was being pursued.

Half a dozen passengers and the guard—none of them pressed for time—joined in the hue and cry.

What it was all about I cannot imagine; all I know is that that evening, in the meadows near C—, a wretched Cockney, in a battered chimney-pot hat, and carrying an umbrella, was wantonly run to earth by a handful of natives, and that an hour later the same unhappy person was clapped in the village lock-up for the night as a suspicious character! It had all been tending to this. Fate had marked me for her own, and run me down at last. Perhaps I *was* a criminal after all, and did not know it. At any rate, I was too fatigued to care much what happened. I "reserved my defence," as they say in the police courts, and resigned myself to spend the night as comfortably as possible in the comparative seclusion of a small apartment which, whatever may have been its defects, compared most favourably with the cabin in which I had lain the night before.

It was about ten o'clock next morning before I had an opportunity of talking my case over with the inspector, and suggesting to him he had better let me go. He, good fellow, at once fell in with my wishes, after hearing my statement, and in his anxiety to efface any unpleasant impressions, I suppose, proposed an adjournment to the "Hotel" to drink "siccess to the ould counthree."

The proposed toast was not sufficiently relevant to the business I had on hand to allure me, so I made my excuses and hastened to the telegraph office to ascertain whether they had any message for me there.

They had. It was from my manager, as I expected; but the contents were astounding—

"Return at once. Robber captured here. Keep down expenses."

Talbot Baines Reed

It would be hard to say which of these three important sentences struck me as the most cruel. I think the last.

I was standing in the street, staring blankly at the missive, when I was startled beyond measure by feeling a hand on my shoulder, and a voice pronouncing my name—

"Samuels!"

It was Michael McCrane. But not the Michael McCrane I knew in the City, or the one I had seen going below on board the steamer. He wore a frock-coat and light trousers, lavender gloves, and a hat—glorious product of that identical box—in which you might see your own face. A rose was in his button-hole, his hair was brushed, his collar was white, and his chin was absolutely smooth.

"Whatever are you doing here?" he asked.

"Oh," faltered I, for I was fairly overcome, both by my own misfortunes and his magnificent appearance, "nothing; only a—a little business run, you know, for the manager."

"I didn't know we had any customers in these parts."

"Well no. But, I say, what are *you* doing here?"

"Business too," said he—"grave business. By the way, Samuels, have you got any better clothes than these?"

Here was a question. And from Michael McCrane!

"Because," he went on—and here he became embarrassed himself—"if you had—in fact, you'd do as you are, because you won't have to wear your hat. What I mean is, that now you *are* here—I'd be awfully obliged if you'd be my best man—I'm to be married this morning. I say, there's the bell beginning to ring. Come on, Samuels."

Talbot Baines Reed

CHAPTER TEN

NEW LIGHT ON AN OLD FABLE

PART I

A DISCOVERY

What cannot one discover on an old bookstall? Who would have supposed I should have had the luck to pick up the extraordinary collection of newspaper-cuttings which are here presented to the reader?

The extracts speak for themselves. They present in a moderately connected form the story of a famous epoch in English history, and shed a flood of light on transactions which have long since passed into the region of myth.

Although the dates of months and days are given, the actual year to which the extracts refer is unfortunately left in obscurity. But from internal evidence, and certain references to current events, it is supposed that the date cannot have been later than the reign of King Arthur—or at any rate before the Saxon period.

I may say that in reading over the present account and the

mythological story of Jack the Giant Killer, I am struck by several discrepancies in the commonly received tradition, and in the account of the manners and customs of the times here revealed. I make no attempt to reconcile the two versions, though I am decidedly of opinion that of the two the present may be accepted by the reader as the more authentic.

At any rate it is an editor's duty to give his story as he receives it, and to leave his readers to form their own conclusions.

The following, then, is an exact transcript of the newspaper extracts to which we have referred:

From the *Stilly Gazette*, June 30th.

Despatches from the mainland report that the season is now in full swing. The charming seaside resorts on this attractive coast are crowded with visitors. It is remarked, as a singular indication of the uncertainties attending excursion traffic, that the proportion of arrivals is greatly in advance of the departures. This is particularly noticeable in the neighbourhood of Giants' Bay, where the well-known hospitality of the residents appears to have an extraordinary fascination for visitors. It is rumoured that although fresh arrivals take place daily, and no departures are announced, the number of visitors remains comparatively stationary, and the place has at no time been inconveniently crowded. Altogether there seems to be every prospect of a prosperous season.

From the *Giants Bay Broadsheet*, July 2nd.

Fashionable Arrivals.—Giant Blunderbore's Hotel: Sir Cap a Pie, Lady a Pie, the Misses a Pie, Master Hugh a Pie, and suite, from London; the Reverend Simon Cellarer, from

Lincoln; Monsieur et Madame Froggi and infant, from Rouen, etcetera, etcetera.

Giant Cormorants Hotel: Fifty members of the West Anglian Anthropomorphic Society, under the conduct of Professor Hardhide.

Giant Galligantus's Hotel: Eighty-two visitors have arrived within the last two days. There will be vacancies in a week.

Notice.—The band will play daily in Blunderbore Park. Public receptions by the Giants in the pump-room every afternoon. Private "At Homes" every evening. Applications should be made early.

Departure.—Since our last report one visitor has left Giants' Bay. As he omitted to discharge his hotel bill, we forbear, pending proceedings, to publish his name.

From the *West Anglian Anthropomorphism*, July 1st.

A party of fifty of our members, under the distinguished conduct of Professor Hardhide, our President, have gone to explore the natural and animal beauties of Giants' Bay. It is expected that the excursion will result in much valuable information respecting the celebrated tall men of that famous resort. Our colleagues, we understand, are occupying Giant Cormoran's commodious hotel, and are much delighted with the arrangements made by their genial host for their comfort. A meeting of the society is summoned for September 1st, to hear the report of their interesting investigations.

From the *Rouen Weekly Supplement*, July 1st.

Nous avons l'honneur d'annoncer que nos concitoyens distingues, Monsieur Alphonse Froggi, avec sa charmante femme et jolie enfant sont partis hier par le paquet. On dit que leur destination est la Baie des Geantes, a l'Angleterre, ou ils resteront a l'Hotel Geant Blunderbore.

From the *London Times*, July 1st.

Major-General Sir Cap a Pie has been ordered for his health to the south coast, and leaves to-day, with family and suite, for Giant Blunderbore's Hotel, Giants' Bay.

From the *Lincoln Daily Gossip*, June 30th.

After a season of unusual fatigue we are happy to be able to announce that our eloquent townsman, the Reverend Simon Cellarer, has at last decided to give himself a long-earned rest, and has left this day (Tuesday) for Cornwall, where he will spend a few weeks in seclusion at Giants' Bay. The reverend gentleman has, we are glad to say, taken his tricycle with him.

From the *Excursionist's Guide*.

Advertisement.—Cheap Daily Excursions. Special facilities. Return tickets at the price of single. Magnificent air. Sea bathing. Fine hotels—Blunderbore, Cormoran and Galligantus. Hundreds of visitors daily.

From the *Scampingtonian* (the Holiday Number of the Scampington School Magazine).

The following from a Pie minor will be read with interest by our readers:—

"Blunderbore's, Giants' Bay."

"Dear Chappies,—I don't think much of Cornwall. The

gingerbeer's beastly bad, and there's not a single chap here can play tennis. The bathing's only so so, and not a boat to be had except an old barge, which Blunderbore uses as a skiff. He's a regular rum Johnny, old Blunderbore; stands about 18 feet in his stockings, 108 inches round the chest, and got a voice to match. He's the boss of this place, and tries to be civil, people say. There's a jolly mixed lot at this hotel. A French chap who doesn't know his own language, at least he pretended not to when I talked to him and said, 'Il regarde comme un mouille jour.' Any ass would know what that meant; you would yourselves. Then there's a lot of old fogies who belong to a society or something, and go and measure, old Blunderbore round the chest and biceps, and photograph him, and all sorts of tomfoolery. How'd they like it themselves? They say they're working in the interests of science. I'd like to catch any one working in the interests of science on my biceps! Rather a rum go yesterday. The governor and mater were asked to an 'At Home' at Blunderbore's private house. I was asked too, but backed out. They went in full toggery, and haven't turned up again at the hotel. I asked Blunderbore, and he said he saw the last of them about eleven last night, and was very sorry when their visit came to an end. I suppose they've gone and lost themselves on the way home. I shall have to go and look for them. Blunderbore wants me to go to his next party, but I shall get out of it if I can. Ta, ta, chappies. It's jolly slow here. The only lively chap is a parson from Lincoln with a tricycle; also a medical fellow just turned up called Jack, a sort of dark horse, who doesn't talk to anybody.

"Yours ever,—"

"Hugh a Pie."

"'P.S.—The fellow called Jack is a swell with the boxing-gloves. He doubled me up in two rounds, and it's not everybody could do that.'"

From the *West Anglian Anthropomorphist*, July 10th. [A communication from the learned President.]

I anticipate the more detailed account of this singular neighbourhood, which I hope to make when I address you at the meeting on September 1st, by a few preliminary notes on some most extraordinary anthropological discoveries which certain members of the society have recently made among the inhabitants of Giants' Bay. At a very early period of the world's history, midway, it is conjectured, between the glacial and basaltic epochs—that is to say, about 100,000 years before the creation of the world—there appears to have prevailed an unusual divergence in the normal stature of the mammal bipeds in the county of Cornwall.

Fossil remains indicate the primeval existence of an under-sized race whose average height has been ascertained to be 4 feet 8.30562 inches. This precise figure has been calculated by a member of this society, from the measurement of an apparently human footprint discovered in the chalk deposit thrown up in course of the erection of a public lamp, in the vicinity of the Assembly Room. As the heavy rains of the last few days have unfortunately obliterated this interesting impression, the society is to be congratulated on the prescience of the member who was energetic enough to measure it while still existent.

In contrast to this diminutive race we have discovered traces of a gigantic race, still in existence. Three of these remarkable beings inhabit this locality, where they occupy high positions as proprietors of the leading hostelries of the place. Indeed, I *may* say that the members of the society at the present time at Giants' Bay have the good fortune to be quartered on the premises of one of these singular specimens of a mammoth prehistoric civilisation. An opportunity is about to be given to each member singly to inspect the phenomenon thus opportunely brought under observation.

It need hardly be stated that the collaboration of the individual reports which it is proposed to make promises to result in one of the most important contributions to anthropological science which has ever been placed on record. The preliminary inspection is to be made by the president to-morrow; and it is expected that the complete report will be ready for the public about the end of the month.

From the *Giants Bay Broadsheet*, July 10th.

Fashionable Arrival.—Blunderbore Hotel: John Smith, M.D.; no address.

Announcement.—The band will play every evening in the hall of Blunderbore Hall, during the receptions. Applications for private interviews should be made at once. Owing to the unusual number desirous of an introduction, Giant Blunderbore will not be open to make any fresh appointment for a fortnight, when priority will be given to the first applicant.

Departure.—A few visitors have already left the bay, including Major- General Sir Cap a Pie and lady, who, however, have left their family at the Blunderbore Hotel, and are expected to return. Monsieur and Madame Froggi also remain, but their infant has departed.

From the *Stilly Gazette*, July 15th.

Our Giants' Bay correspondent reports a steadily maintained influx of visitors. As a proof of the popularity of this Elysian spot, it may be remarked that only one visitor has left within the last fortnight.

From the *Evening Tell-Tale*, London, July 15th.

Mysterious Affair at a Seaside Watering-Place.—

Disappearance of a Lincoln Clergyman.—A remarkable rumour reaches us from Giants' Bay. Among the numerous visitors to this popular place of resort during the last fortnight was the Reverend Simon Cellarer, an eminent divine hailing from Lincoln. Mr Cellarer, who travelled to Giants' Bay on his tricycle, and was staying at the Blunderbore Grand Hotel, has, it appears, been missing since the 8th inst., when he was seen in his usual good health and spirits exercising on his machine in the grounds of the hotel.

As abrupt departures are not uncommon at seaside places of resort, no notice of his absence appears to have been taken for a day or two. On his failure to return, however, after three days, inquiries were at once instituted, and the reverend gentleman's tricycle was found, apparently undamaged, in the grounds. Further search was rewarded by the discovery of his boots and spectacles in the vicinity: but up to the time of going to press we have no intelligence that the gentleman himself has come to light.

From the *London Times*, July 18th.

Advertisement.—Lost, strayed, or stolen, a father and mother, answering to the name of Sir Cap and Lady a Pie. Respectable, well-dressed, quiet manners. Last seen at Blunderbore Hotel, Giants' Bay, July 8th. The former was in full armour. Any one giving information as to what they are up to will receive half a crown reward. If they return, all shall be forgiven.—Apply to Hugh a Pie, at the above address.

Talbot Baines Reed

From the *Giants Bay Broadsheet*, July 20th.

Giant Blunderbore is, we regret to say, indisposed. He is suffering from a sharp attack of dyspepsia. For the present his receptions will be suspended. Giants Cormoran and Galligantus, though also to some extent sufferers from the same complaint, have very kindly undertaken to receive visitors daily from two till eight.

Notice.—In future, no one in armour, or occupying the office of president of any learned society, will be admitted.

From the *Evening Tell-Tale*, July 22th.

The Giants' Bay Mystery.—

Alleged Further Disappearances.—

Extraordinary Rumours.—Up to the present time no trace has been found of the missing clergyman at Giant's Bay. Sinister rumours prevail of other persons being missing, including a distinguished military gentleman and his lady, and a foreign infant. The police we understand, do not attach much importance to this or any other rumour.

From the *Lincoln Weekly Supplement*, July 22th.

Great gloom has fallen over this otherwise cheerful city in consequence of the rumoured disappearance of our esteemed and reverend townsman, the Reverend Simon Cellarer, from Giants' Bay.

With its usual enterprise, the *Supplement* has despatched a special commissioner to the scene of the mystery, with instructions to interview the leading persons in the place, including the giants, and make a full report of the circumstances attending the abrupt disappearance of the reverend missing one.

Full particulars may be expected in our next; which, to meet the demands of our numerous readers, will be charged twopence instead of a penny. It is proposed to reserve one sheet for advertisements. Applications for space should be made at once.

From the *Anthropomorphist*, July 25th.

We regret to say we are unable to publish a further instalment of the report of the deeply interesting investigations being made at the present time by our members in Giants' Bay.

Contrary to expectation, no communication has been received for several days. We shall endeavour to accommodate the extra matter which may be expected in our next by issuing a double number, which will be charged one shilling instead of sixpence. In response to numerous requests we beg to intimate that a limited number of advertisements will be inserted, for which application should be made at once.

Talbot Baines Reed

PART II

From the *Stilly Gazette*, July 24th.

We understand that the last arrival at Giants' Bay has been our talented young fellow-islander Dr John Smith. Dr Smith has arrived at the Bay at an opportune time, as we hear that Giant Blunderbore is ill, and will doubtless avail himself of his guest's well-known professional services.

From the *Giants' Bay Broadsheet*, July 27th.

The following bulletin has been issued: "Giant Blunderbore is still suffering from the effects of his recent sharp attack of indigestion; but is better. His appetite is good; and he feels able to resume his receptions."

Later.—Giant Blunderbore has had a slight relapse, and some anxiety is felt as to his condition. Dr Smith, of Scilly, at present resident in the hotel, has been called in, and a consultation is about to take place. Meanwhile Giants Cormoran and Galligantus are prepared to receive visitors daily at 3 and 8 p.m.

From the *Evening Tell-Tale*, July 28th.

The Missing Tourists.—

Extraordinary Rumours.—No News of the Lincoln Clergyman.—

Fifty Scientific Men Missing.—The most astonishing rumours continue to come in from Giants' Bay. In addition to the disappearance recorded in a recent issue, we have received information that a whole congress of anthropomorphists has been missing for a week. They were quartered at Cormoran's Hotel, where their personal effects still remain.

Many conjectures are afloat, the most reasonable of which appears to point to the probability of the unfortunate tourists having been engulfed in the sands, which at certain states of the tide are said to be highly dangerous along this coast.

Later.—At the Round Table to-night a question was asked as to the extraordinary disappearances reported from Giants' Bay. The Home Secretary requested the hon, member to give notice of the question for this day week.

From the *Giants Bay Broadsheet*, July 28th.

The following bulletins have been issued:—

12:30 p.m.—Giant Blunderbore is decidedly worse. Contrary to medical advice, he partook of a hearty meal last night. Dr Smith is still in attendance.

4 p.m.—Giant Blunderbore lies in a hopeless state. He has again disregarded medical advice, and eaten solid food. Dr Smith is still in attendance.

8 p.m.—It is with the deepest regret that we have to announce the death of our esteemed patron Giant Blunderbore, which took place suddenly this evening, after a somewhat painful operation. Details are not yet forthcoming; but we expect to issue an extra double number to-morrow, with a coloured photograph of the deceased. As only a limited number will be printed, copies should be ordered early. The attention of advertisers is drawn to the present unusual opportunity.

Latest.—Just as we go to press we hear that Dr Smith has

Talbot Baines Reed

been summoned to attend Giant Cormoran, who is ailing of a complaint which presents symptoms similar to those of the late Giant Blunderbore.

From the *Scampingtonian*, July 27th.

Dear Chappies,—No end of a go! Can't find my people high or low. People been sloping off all round. Fancy I know why now. On Monday I saw Blunderbore's door open as I passed, and I thought I'd pop in and see what he knew about it. He was sitting in his chair, looking jolly blue.

"What's up, Blundy?" I said.

"I'm awfully hungry," said he.

"Why don't you have some grub?" I said.

"Doctors won't let me," said he. "You see, a week ago I happened to eat something that disagreed with me. Between me and you," said he, "it was a knight in armour. I didn't mind the knight, but the armour gave me a very bad turn."

"Do you know," said I, "that was my governor?"

"My dear boy," said he, "I'm awfully sorry. I feel for you. I wish I hadn't done it—sincerely. But a fellow must live. Really, I sympathise with you; let me grasp your hand."

"Not if I know it, you cad," said I; "and where's my mother?"

"That's another thing that troubles me," said he. "Tell me, did she wear a brocaded silk gown with beads? Most unlucky for us both! Beads never did agree with me. It's a warning to both of us to be more particular. Really, you *must* let me grasp your hand."

"Not much!" said I. "Look here, Blunderbore, I mean to show you up. I'll let some of our fellows know about you, and you see if they don't make you sit up before long."

"I feel much more like lying down," said he. "Would you mind handing me that medicine bottle?"

"Don't you wish *you* may get it!" said I, and cut.

I told Jack Smith about it, and he was no end riled. I must say, I feel riled myself. It's specially awkward, because the mater had our return tickets in her pocket; and I can't get away from here. I wish you'd send me a sov., some of you. I'll square up after vac.

Yours ever, Hugh a Pie.

P.S.—Here's a go! Old Blunderbore's gone at last! Smith says it was the steel armour inside him that did it. Serves him jolly well right!

From the *Giants' Bay Broadsheet*, July 29th.

It is with feelings almost akin to consternation that we announce the sudden and critical illness of our esteemed fellow-citizen Giant Cormoran. The regret with which we make this announcement will be shared by all those visitors to this charming retreat who during the last months have come into contact with the amiable and accommodating gentleman.

Giant Cormoran is one of the old school of Englishmen whom we can ill afford to lose. Capacious in mind and body, with a large sense of humour, of strict personal integrity, and a hearty enjoyment of life, it is indeed sad to think of him at the present moment as lying on a bed of languishing, from which it is doubtful whether he will rise more. Very little news leaks out from the sick-chamber. Dr Smith is in regular attendance, and, according to a curt bulletin published an hour ago, reports his patient's condition as exceedingly grave: "Giant Cormoran is in a state of collapse. There is a complete loss of nervous power. The patient has quite lost his head."

We have no doubt that the melancholy death of his comrade Giant Blunderbore has seriously affected his nerves. Happily, his condition spares him the additional pang of knowing that Giant Galligantus is also on the sick list, with what it is feared is a mild attack of the prevailing epidemic. Later.

The following bulletins have just appeared: "The condition of Giant Cormoran remains unchanged.

"John Smith, M.D."

"Giant Galligantus is suffering from a severe shock to the system, with complications. It is feared that the attack is of a similar nature to that of Giants Blunderbore and Cormoran.

"John Smith, M.D."

Latest.—Giant Cormoran is no more. A memoir will appear in our next. Special space will be reserved for advertisements on the cover.

From the *Evening Tell-Tale*, August 1st.

The Giants' Bay Mysteries.—

The Plot Thickens.—

Sudden Death of Giants.—

Rumoured Government Intervention.—

Further Wholesale Disappearances.—The plot thickens at Giants' Bay. Two of the leading giants of the place, Giants Blunderbore and Cormoran, have died of what is apparently an acute gastric epidemic. Meanwhile hundreds of inquiries are pouring into the place respecting missing relatives and friends. It is stated that an entire learned society has disappeared.

Owing to the urgent representations of the *Tell-Tale* and other journals, the Government has at last awakened to a sense of the gravity of the situation. At the Round Table last night a commission was appointed to inquire into the matter. It will meet this day week, and after appointing president and secretary, adjourn till October.

The police are reticent; but on inquiry at the head office we understand that search is being made in the atlas for Giants' Bay. For the information of our readers, we give a map of the locality of the mysteries, and fancy portraits of the three giants. During the present excitement, and in the interests of our subscribers, it has been decided permanently to double the price of the *Tell-Tale*.

From the *West Anglian Anthropomorphist*, August 2nd.

In the continued unexplained absence of the president and members of the society, the usual meetings will not be held in August. We may point out for the benefit of advertisers that a considerable amount of additional space will thus be available for their announcements.

From the *Giants' Bay Broadsheet*, August 3rd.

Talbot Baines Reed

It is with feelings of unfeigned melancholy that we announce the demise of our excellent neighbour Giant Galligantus, after a brief illness. The lamented giant never rallied from the nervous shock which overtook him a few days since. Although details are still a-wanting, we understand that his head was seriously affected. Dr John Smith was in attendance to the last. Further particulars, with an extra supplement and portrait memoirs of the three giants, will be given in our next. In order not to disappoint our readers and advertisers, the prices in each department will be further doubled.

Departure.—John Smith, Esquire, M.D., has left Giants' Bay.

From the *Hue and Cry*, August 14th. Police Notice.

Whereas several persons have recently disappeared from the neighbourhood of Giants' Bay, in the county of Cornwall, a reward of One Pound will be offered to any person, not a principal, who shall give any information leading to the detection of the aforesaid.

From the *Evening Tell-Tale*, August 6th.

Our special correspondent at Giants' Bay writes: "The excitement here is unabated. All sorts of conjectures are afloat. General opinion seems to connect the wholesale disappearance of tourists and the sudden death of the three giants as parts of the fiendish scheme of some person unknown. The miscreant is supposed to be interested in some other watering-place.

"We have been fortunate enough to secure a personal interview with the celebrated Dr John Smith, whose remarks—in view of his recent close personal relations with the deceased giants—will be read with interest. We found the youthful doctor enjoying a fragrant weed in the verandah of his father's bijou residence in Scilly.

"'A beautiful day, doctor,' we said, taking the vacant seat beside him."

"'Is it?' replied he, placing his two feet in a graceful attitude on the elaborately-polished balustrade of the balcony."

"'Heard of you at Giants' Bay,' we remarked, by way of leading up to the subject. There was a pause, and then the doctor replied, 'Oh!'"

"'A strange affair the sudden mortality in that place, doctor.'"

"'What about it?' was the unexpected rejoinder, as the man of physic slowly assumed a standing attitude."

"He was dressed in a light check suit, which reflected considerable credit on the provincial tailor who made it."

"'That's the question,' we replied, with a touch of humour."

"The doctor appeared to feel the heat, but presently recovered sufficiently to call our attention to the peculiar make of his boots. They were large, with flapped uppers and clumped soles, and could hardly have cost less than a guinea the pair. We congratulated him warmly upon his possession. Dr Smith was evidently proud of them."

"'See them?' said he, pointing to the right foot."

"We nodded a friendly assent, inwardly amused at our friend's eccentricity."

"'Do you see that hill there?' said he, abruptly pointing over our shoulder."

Talbot Baines Reed

"We turned to look. It was indeed a fine view which met our eyes—a view of which any native of Scilly might be proud. We were about to make an observation to the effect, when he interrupted us."

"'Feel them?'"

We certainly did feel something—not in front of us—and not being anxious to take up more of our friend's valuable time, we thanked him for his courtesy and retired.

From the *Round Table Hansard*, August 25th.

Giants' Bay Select Committee.—Lord Merlin was in the chair. The committee sat for a short time to draw up rules of procedure and arrange an adjournment. It was decided to prorogue the inquiry for six months, in order to allow witnesses to attend. A brief discussion ensued on the question of costs, and a short Bill was drafted, which it is proposed to add to the estimates.

The Chairman expressed an opinion that an additional two-pence on the income-tax would amply cover the costs of the commission; and it was agreed to await the passing of the Bill before fixing the date for the next meeting. The committee then adjourned.

From the *Giants' Bay Broadsheet*, September 10th.

Preliminary Notice.—On the 1st of April next, at the Mart, will be sold those three eligible hotels—namely, Blunderbore Hotel, Cormoran Hotel, and Galligantus Hotel, pleasantly situated in Giants' Bay, Cornwall, commanding fine views of the sea. These palatial houses, standing in their own grounds, are fitted with every comfort and replete with every convenience. Fixtures at a valuation. By order of the executors of the late Giants Blunderbore, Cormoran, and Galligantus.

Catalogues and orders to view on application.

From the *Army Gazetteer*, December 1st.

Captain Tom Thumb to be Major-General, *vice* Sir Cap a Pie, deceased.

From the *Lincoln Weekly Supplement*, December 25th.

The Reverend Friar Tucker has been appointed to the living lately held by the Reverend Simon Cellarer.

From the *West Anglian Anthropomorphist*, January 1st.

At a meeting held last week it was decided to reorganise this society. A new president was elected. It was announced that an exhibition would be offered yearly, to be called the "Hardhide Exhibition," for the best essay on the gigantic remains of south-west Britain.

From the *Scampingtonian*, January 25th.

Term has begun. We are glad to say that our chum, a Pie— now Sir Hugh a Pie—has been unanimously elected captain of the football club.

From the *Stilly Gazette*, April 3rd.

At the mart on Monday were sold the three Giant Hotels of Giants' Bay. The bidding was very slack, but we understand the lots were eventually knocked down to a dealer in old bricks.

Our respected fellow-islander, Dr John Smith, has had the honour of being presented at court, where his Majesty has been pleased to confer on him several stripes, and the order of the Giant Killer. A public reception is to be held in the market-place to welcome home Sir John Smith, G.K., M.D., on his return from London.

From the *Giants' Bay Broadsheet*, June 1st.

The offices of this paper being now closed, subscribers are requested to forward outstanding accounts by return to Messrs. Payup and Shellout, Solicitors, London.

CHAPTER ELEVEN

SUB-CHAPTER I

THE COASTGUARDSMAN'S YARN

A LEGEND OF THE CIVIL WAR

Several summers ago I happened to be spending a few weeks at W—, a small fishing village on the Welsh coast. A beautiful little place it was, nestling in a break of the cliffs which rose majestically above it on either side and stretched in gaunt rugged walls seaward.

The beautiful bay, with its sunset lights behind the grand headland, with its deep caves and tumbled rocks, and above all its blue waters, lying sometimes calm and motionless, and at others dashing furiously at the foot of the cliffs, was enough to attract any lover of nature.

And dull little place as it was, with its one tiny inn and its handful of natives, the time I spent there, with my easel and paint-brush, was one of the most enjoyable of my life.

But beautiful as the view was from the land, I found the view from the sea still more attractive, and in order to gratify my tastes in this respect, I took pains to get myself into the good graces of one or two of the fishermen, a few of whom could speak English, and many times accompanied them on their fishing cruises in the bay, where, while they toiled at the nets, I sat and drank in the thousand beauties of the coast, or worked eagerly with my brush to commit them to canvas.

The expedition I liked best was towards the southern headland of the bay, where the cliffs were tallest and steepest and where, to add to the other attractions of the view, stood, perched like an eagle's nest on the edge of the crag, the ruins of an old castle.

By old, I do not mean Roman or even Norman. Indeed in that sense it was comparatively modern; for the building, what was left of it, looked more like one of those Tudor manor-houses which dot the country still, than a fortress. And yet, that it had been fortified was plain enough even still. On the side towards the sea it needed no protection; indeed looking up at it from below, it seemed almost to overhang its precipitous foundation. But on the land side there remained traces of a moat, and loop-holes in the walls, and a massive gate.

It was scarcely to be called a picturesque ruin, except inasmuch as every ruin is picturesque. Its bare walls rose gaunt and black out of the ground, not out of a heap of tumbled moss-grown masonry, or covered over with ivy. There were very few signs of decay about the place, ruinous as it was, and very little examination was enough to show that it had suffered not from old age, or from the cannon of an enemy, but from fire.

No one about could tell me its story, and the mystery of the place only added to its charm. Indeed I was quite glad to discover that it had not even a name, and that the country folk would as soon have thought of crossing the old moat after nightfall as they would have done of stepping over the edge of the cliff. The only thing I could learn about it, in fact, was that it was haunted, and that the one little turret which still retained a roof, and over which the only ivy visible tried to creep, was railed the Lady Tower, and was the "most haunted" spot of all.

I could not believe that the one corner of the old ruin where there still remained a sign of life and verdure, could be infested by any very terrible ghost. Still I am not quite sure whether I should have enjoyed a solitary night's rest there, and to have suggested the thing to the natives of W—would have been enough to secure my incarceration as a raving lunatic. So I did not. But by daytime I added myself one more to the spirits that haunted the place, and yielded myself up completely to its fascination.

One day towards the end of my visit I walked over to a coastguard station some miles along the shore for the sake of taking a last survey of the beautiful coast. When I reached it I found, to my pleasure, one of the W—fishing-boats just preparing to put out and sail round the headland back to the village. One of the coastguardsmen was on board, and I was glad to accept the invitation of my honest friend to form another of the party.

I found the coastguardsman a most intelligent fellow—well informed on many subjects, and even professing to be something of an art critic. I showed him one or two of my pictures, and he was graciously pleased to approve of them, especially a sketch of the ruined castle from the south, with the Lady Tower in the foreground.

The examination of this picture naturally turned the conversation on to the ruin, and I was delighted to find my

Talbot Baines Reed

companion seemed almost as interested in the subject as I was.

"It's a strange thing," said I, "that the one thing wanting seems to be a story."

"Ah! that was burnt out by the fire, sir."

I was rude enough to laugh. He fancied I was lamenting the absence of the top storey!

"I don't mean that," I said. "What I mean is, no one seems to know anything about the place or its history."

"Not they! What should they bother their heads about it for?"

"But it must have a history of some sort," said I.

"Of course it has."

"Do you know it?"

"Of course I do."

It was quite a shock to me to find any one knew anything about my ruin, and it was some time before I ventured to ask—

"Would you tell it to me?"

Instead of saying "Yes," the coastguardsman laid down his telescope, pulled a plug of tobacco out of his pocket, and, cutting off a small quid, put it into his mouth, looked up at the sail, shifted himself once or twice in his seat, and then, looking to see if I was ready, began—

"It's not such a wonderful yarn after all, sir. You see, something like two hundred and fifty years ago, when our Civil Wars were going on—you've heard of them, I suppose?—yonder castle belonged to a stout Charles the First's man called Fulke. He owned a good bit about this coast, I'm told, and the folk at the New Manor are sort of descendants. But direct descendants they can't be, for Fulke only had one daughter, sir, and she never married. If it hadn't been for those cruel wars she would have been married, though, for she was betrothed to a neighbour, young Morgan, who lived beyond that hill there, and mightily they loved one another too! Fulke, whose lands joined on Morgan's, was pleased enough to have the two families united, and united they would have been to this day but for the Civil Wars. I'm no great hand at dates, sir, but it was somewheres about 1642 that things began to get unpleasant.

"One day, not long before the wedding was to be, Fulke and his daughter went over to Morgan Hall; and while the young folk spent the day love- making in the garden the two old folk sat and discussed the affairs of the nation in the house. And it's safe to say the two out of doors agreed far better than the two indoors. For Morgan went with the Parliament, and told Fulke the King had no right to try and arrest the five members, and that the Parliament had done a fine thing in protecting them, and that if he'd been there he'd have called out against the King as loud as any of them. At that Fulke—who was a hot- headed man at best of times, and who went mad to hear any one say a word against the King—got up in a rage, and, taking his hat, stalked out into the garden, and taking his daughter by the arm marched away from Morgan Hall with never a word.

"It was a sad business. The young folks begged and the old Morgan sent a letter; but no, Fulke wouldn't listen to one of them, and forbade his daughter to leave the castle."

Talbot Baines Reed

"Whether the lovers saw one another after that I don't know, but almost directly after the war blazed out and the whole country went mad. Morgan and his son had to leave these parts, and took arms under the Parliament, while Fulke brought guns and powder into his castle, and hoisted the flag of King Charles."

"The young lady had a busy time of it sheltering and entertaining the Royalists who came this way. But she had no heart in it—not that she didn't love the King, sir. Yet she loved young Morgan more."

"So things went on for four or live years. The King, as you know, sir, got the worst of it, and was driven to his wits' end. Most of his friends had fallen, and some had deserted. But so far no one had given Fulke much trouble. Either they had never heard of him, or saw there was not much to fear from him. So the Royal flag waved over the castle day and night, and the young lady did what her father bid her, and never went abroad or heard a word of young Morgan.

"But at last the King, not knowing what to do, tried to bring over the Irish to help him. And then it was the troubles in these parts began. For every one that was suspected of aiding in this venture was doomed by the Parliament."

"And Fulke was suspected. Rightly or wrongly I can't say, but I've a notion there was something in it. Anyway, his castle commanded the bay, and the Parliament made up their minds to have it. Fulke had only time to get a score or so of men with arms and provender inside his gate, when a troop of roundheads came with their guns over the lulls and sat down before it.

"The leader of the troop was a Colonel Frank, a cruel, ruffianly fellow, as you shall hear. And the second in command was no other than young Captain Morgan himself.

"He had had plenty of rough work during the war, and had done it well. And it's a pity, sir, all the Parliament's officers weren't of his sort, for he was as unlike Colonel Frank as a house-dog is to a wolf. When first ordered on this expedition he didn't know where he was going, and you can fancy his horror at finding out that he was to lay siege to the very castle that held his lady-love. At first he would have held back, and even refused. But he was under iron rules, and besides, thought he, I might help my lady more by going than staying away.

"So he came with the troop to the castle, and looked wistfully up at the little turret yonder, and prayed that she might never know that he was where he was.

"Colonel Frank came expecting an easy task with this small out-of-the- way castle. But it was not so easy as he thought. On two sides, as you see, sir, no mortal man could get at it. And on the other two, Fulke had guarded himself so well that by the end of a fortnight the Roundheads were not an inch nearer getting the place than they had been when they began.

"The rage of the colonel knew no bounds, and he vowed all sorts of vengeance. You may fancy one of his men did not join in his threats. Many a time that fortnight Captain Morgan wished a shot from the castle might find him out and end his misery. And yet whenever he was tempted to desert or quarrel with his colonel the thought of the lady left with no protector at the mercy of such a man held him to his post. All he could do was once or twice to urge the colonel to raise the siege, or come to terms with its master. But Frank was bent on vengeance, and at last poor Morgan had to desist for fear of getting suspected himself.

Talbot Baines Reed

"About three weeks after the siege had begun, when the Roundheads were beginning to lose spirit, and Morgan's hopes were beginning to rise once more, a trooper rushed into the colonel's tent to say he had found a small cave below the top of the cliff which seemed to run up under the castle. The colonel's eyes blazed at the news, and he ordered the man to lead him instantly to the spot. Do you see a square grey patch on the face of the cliff up there, sir, nearly at the top, under the south corner?"

"Yes; what is it?"

"That's the mouth of the cave. At least, it's not a cave now, for it's filled up. But it was there the trooper, under cover of night, led the colonel and the captain. They didn't do more than mark the place then, for fear an alarm might be given by a sentinel within."

"'Now,' says Colonel Frank, 'the castle's ours; and not a soul inside it shall be there by this time to-morrow.'"

"'What shall you do?' says Captain Morgan, pale, and with a shaky voice."

"'Do? Art thou a dunce, Morgan? Without doubt, at the end of that cave is a way up into the castle; and though the passage be too narrow for all my troop, three men and a captain will suffice to lay faggots and light them at the door. What say you, comrade?'"

"'What!' cries Morgan, 'would you burn the place? No, no, colonel; we will capture it if we can, but it is no soldier's work to burn men in their beds!'"

"'Fool!' exclaims the colonel, in a passion, 'it is no captain's work to read sermons to his colonel, sirrah! These rebels shall be smoked out like all other vermin!'"

"'But,' says the captain once more, and very pale—'but I hear there is a lady in the castle, and—'"

"'Peace, sir, on your peril!' exclaims the colonel, 'and hold yourself ready to obey orders when I shall give them.'"

It was no use saying more, young Morgan saw that. As it was, he knew his colonel half suspected him of some treachery, and for the rest of that day put a watch upon him. Twenty times that day he was on the point of risking all consequences and declaring to his officer's face he would have no hand in this bad business. But the thought of how much worse that might be for the folk in the castle kept him to his post.

"Well, sir, the day passed, and they kept up a show of besieging the place on the land side, and took care to keep all Fulke's guns turned that way. But at nightfall Colonel Frank called Morgan to him and ordered him to take six men, whom he named, and try the passage."

"'If you find a sentinel at this end,' says the colonel, 'see he is overpowered and taken before an alarm can be given. Over the cliff will be the shortest way with him. The men you take know their business; and see you perform yours!' he says, with a scowl. 'I and the rest of the troop will be ready to storm the place as soon as we see the flames. Go now, lose no time; and, hark you, there is no quarter to-night for traitors!'"

"This last remark may have been meant for the captain, who knew that, at heart, he was a traitor to the Parliament that night; or it may have been meant for the inmates of the castle. Anyway, it sounded ugly enough, and it was all

Talbot Baines Reed

Morgan could do to hold his peace and make no reply."

"He found the six men waiting for him without, and in the darkness they crept stealthily round to the edge of the cliff, where a narrow ledge led down to the end of the cave."

"It was a perilous step down, especially to those unaccustomed to the way. But the spot had been carefully marked in the daytime, and presently the little band all stood there at the entrance. Morgan in his secret heart wished some sentinel of the besieged might have perceived them, and so given an alarm. But no; such was the security Fulke felt in the secrecy of his cave that it never entered his head to guard it."

"The men entered one by one, with a man carrying a light in front. The passage was too narrow to allow of two abreast, and too low for any one to stand upright in it. So, single file, on hands and knees, they crawled forward."

"At last, when they had gone some way, and the sound of the sea grew faint in the distance, Morgan halted his men."

"'Give me the light,' says he, 'and stay here while I go forward and see how the passage ends.'"

"He crawled forward to the front of the file and took the torch from the hands of the foremost man. But when he began to move forward he noticed that two of the band followed him at a short distance."

"'Did I not order you to remain with the rest?' demands he, angrily."

"'Pardon, captain. The colonel bade us keep close to you,' says one of the men, sourly."

"Morgan's blood ran cold in his veins, and his last hope of giving a friendly warning to those in the castle vanished. However, it was no time to quarrel, and he answered, with a forced laugh, 'The colonel flatters me by his attention. But, as he is anxious for my welfare, come on, my men, and keep your eyes on me.'"

"The three went forward, till the cave became so narrow that they could scarcely drag themselves farther. In one place a little chink in the roof let in a faint ray of moonlight from above."

"At length they could get no farther, and Morgan, turning his head, said, 'It's a false scent, after all; the cave leads nowhere!'"

"But at that moment over their heads they heard a sound of feet, and presently of voices. At first they could distinguish nothing, but after a while Morgan's ears caught some words."

"'Pray, master, get you to bed for this one night. The scoundrels can do nothing till the morning.'"

"'I need no rest, I tell you,' said another voice, sternly. 'How stands the provender, Peter?'"

"'It will last three days, master; and the shot will hold out for two. The water, alas! is already exhausted.'"

"'Ah! And my child—how is she?'"

"'In good heart, master; she was sleeping like a child as I passed her room just now.'"

"Morgan could forbear no longer. He turned quickly to his men and said, in a loud voice, which might be heard by the

Talbot Baines Reed

unseen watchers overhead, 'My torch has gone out. Crawl back, one of you, to the rest and bring another, for if the castle is to be fired to-night—'

"There was a startled movement above, which told him his object had been gained. The voices grew silent, and the footsteps moved suddenly. For a moment his two companions did not comprehend what had happened. But it flashed on them soon enough, and they were ready for the emergency.

"One of the two suddenly lit a small ball of hemp saturated in some inflammable substance, which he had carried with him, and, fixing it on to the point of his sword, held it up to the boards above, at the same time that the other drew his pistol and pointed it at Morgan's head.

"Not a word was said, and not one of the three stirred, until a sharp crackling of the wood above told its own tale. The soldier still held up his brand till the place was well alight. Then withdrawing it, and beckoning to his companion, he began to retreat towards the mouth of the cave, saying as he did so, with a mocking laugh—

"'Farewell, master traitor, I doubt not your business keeps you where you are. We shall miss your company.'"

"Morgan did not hear them. He sprang desperately towards the now blazing boards. But it was too late to stay the fire, and the heat and falling embers drove him back."

"Still he could not go, but stayed there half suffocated, determined at least not to desert his post while a glimmer of hope remained."

"In a few moments there was a crash and a shower of sparks

at his feet. The trap-door had fallen in."

"Heedless of the peril or the pain, he sprang once more at the opening, and this time, how he knew not, succeeded in lifting himself into the blazing apartment. Many a time had he been there before in happier days.

"He rushed across to the door and out into the great hall of the castle. Not a man was there to stop him. He heard voices and shouts outside, but the castle seemed to have been left to its fate. There was yet time, thought he, before the flames reached so far, to rush up to his lady's room and save her.

"He sprang up the staircase. Halfway up he saw a figure before him, ascending too. He called, and the man turned suddenly. Morgan knew him in a moment. It was Fulke himself. The old Royalist, seeing himself pursued by a soldier in the dress of a Roundhead, concluded the enemy had already entered his castle, and with the fury of a desperate man, drew his sword and threw himself upon the stranger. Morgan had no time to hesitate. The delay of a moment might cost his lady her life.

"With a rapid pass of his sword, he struck Fulke across the arm, and as the weapon dropped from the old soldier's hand, Morgan rushed past, on towards the lady's chamber."

"Another obstacle still awaited him. This time it was a groom unarmed, who encountered him. He too, defenceless as he was, sprang wildly upon the intruder to dispute the passage. But Morgan put him by with the flat of his sword and crying—"

"'Look to your master below. I will see to the lady,' darted on."

Talbot Baines Reed

"After that it was all like a dream. He was dimly conscious of rushing down those steps shortly after, with a precious burden in his arms. How he struggled through the smoke and fire, or how he kept his feet on that tottering staircase, no one knows. It's enough to say he struggled forward down the stairs and across the hall as far as the outer door, where some one snatched his unharmed burden from his arms and carried her to a place of safety, where already her father, tended by his faithful servant, was recovering consciousness.

"The courtyard by this time was crowded with troopers, Royalist and Roundhead, and above the roar of the flames and the crashing of falling roofs there rose the report of guns and the clash of swords. Morgan, half stunned and like a man in a dream, was standing propped up against a tree a helpless spectator of the scene, when suddenly one of his own men rushed up to him and saluted.

"'The colonel, sir, is dead. He was under yonder wall as it fell. The men, sir, look to you for orders.'

"Morgan sprang to his feet like one electrified."

"'Call the men off,' he cried hoarsely, 'instantly—without another blow, and bring the prisoners to the camp—to me. Lose not a moment, friend.'"

"The order was obeyed. The Roundheads were glad enough to get clear of the tottering walls without being too particular as to who escaped and who was captured."

"Among the prisoners who next morning were reported to the captain as safe were Fulke, his daughter, and one manservant."

"Morgan's heart failed him. He could not, dared not see

them. He ordered them to be kept in safe custody, and, meanwhile, summoned two of his most trusty soldiers to receive orders respecting them.

"That night a small boat was brought round to the bottom of yonder cliff, where you see the little creak, sir. And in it Fulke and the young lady and their servant were rowed secretly to W—, where a fishing-boat waited to carry them to Ireland. That's the story, sir."

"And what became of Morgan?" said I.

"No one heard of him after this affair, sir. And they do say he was punished as a traitor. But whatever the end of him was, he never repented his night's work at the burning of Fulke Castle."

CHAPTER TWELVE

FALLEN AMONG THIEVES

A GRANDFATHER'S YARN

SUB-CHAPTER I

"When I was a young fellow," began my grandfather—

There was a general silence and a settling of ourselves in our seats, as the wavering voice of the old man uttered these magical words.

No one had asked him to tell a story, some of us had almost forgotten that he was sitting there in his big chair, one of the group which crowded round his own Christmas fire at Culverton Manor.

He was an old, old man, was my grandfather. The proverbial "threescore years and ten" was an old story with him, and even the "fourscore" awarded to the strong was receding into the distance. Yet there he sat, in his old straight-back chair, hale and bright, as he looked round on us his descendants, sons and daughters grey-haired already, grandchildren, who some of them were staid heads of families themselves, and the little group of great-grandchildren, who knew as well as any one that when their father's grandfather began to talk of "the days when he was young," it was worth their while to hold their peace and prick up their ears.

"When I was a young fellow," began my grandfather, stroking his old grizzled moustache, "I was a cornet in the Buffs. It was in the year—heigho! my memory's getting rusty!—it was in the year 1803, I believe, when every one was expecting the French over, and I was quartered with my regiment at Ogilby. Ogilby is an inland town, you know, thirty miles from here; and as there was not much immediate danger of Bonaparte dropping in upon us there without good warning, we had a lazy rollicking time of it in that bright little place.

"We young officers, boys that we were, thought it a fine thing to live as grand gentlemen, and spend our pay half a dozen times over in all sorts of extravagances. And, I recollect with sorrow, I was as bad as any of them."

"Our colonel was an easy-going old soldier, who had been a wild blade himself once, and held that it was little use looking too sharply after us, so he didn't look after us at all; and we in consequence did just as we pleased."

"Sometimes we invited all the gentry round to feast with us at mess, and pledged our pay months in advance to load the table with the most costly delicacies. At other times we would sally forth, and out of sheer mischief organise a riot in the town, and end the night with broken heads, and now and then in the lock-up. And when we were tired of this, we got up I know not what gaieties to pass the time.

"As I said, I was as bad as any of them—worse perhaps. For I had had a good home and careful training, and knew all the time I was joining in the excesses of my comrades that I was a fool and a prodigal, and a traitor to my better self. And yet I went in, and might have gone on to the end of the chapter, had not an event happened to me which served to pull me up short.

"One evening that winter our festivities culminated by a grand entertainment given by the officers of our mess to all the countryside. Compared with this, our former efforts in the same direction had been mere child's play. We had hired the largest assembly room in the town, and decorated it regardless of all expense. The wine merchants and confectioners for miles round had been exhausted to furnish our supper, and the tailors and milliners driven nearly distracted over our toilets. Ogilby had never seen such a brilliant entertainment, and the officers of the Buffs had never achieved such a triumph.

"I was among the last to leave the gay scene, and as I stepped out into the chill winter air, and called for my horse, the clock of the church was striking four. My man had to help me to my saddle, for, what with the sudden change of air, added to the excesses of the evening, I was not steady enough to do it myself. My man was the son of an old tenant of my father's, and as he had known me from childhood, I was used to allowing him more familiarity than most gentlemen allow to their servants. I was, therefore, not surprised when, on reaching my quarters, after helping me to alight, he stopped a moment to speak to me before I entered the house.

"'By your leave, Master Hal,' said he, saluting, 'I thought you might like to know there is bad news from Culverton.'"

"'How?' I demanded, scarcely taking in what he said."

"'Bad news, begging your honour's pardon. I had it in a letter from Phoebe, the dairymaid at the Vicarage, who your honour may know is my sweetheart, or rather I am hers; and by your—'"

"'Sirrah, man, drop your sweetheart and come to your news! What is it?'"

"'It is news of the squire, Master Hal!' said the man, seriously."

"'My father!' I exclaimed, suddenly sobered by the name."

"'He is ill, please your honour. He had a stroke a week ago, and Phoebe says his life is despaired of.'"

"'Ill a week, and I never heard!' I exclaimed. 'Why did no one tell me?'"

"'Your honour may remember you have not examined your letters for these three days past.'"

"It was true. In the whirl of excitement, with late nights and later mornings, and never-ending frivolity, my very letters had lain on my mantelshelf unopened!"

"My man turned to take my horse away to the stable. His action recalled me suddenly to myself."

"'Hold!' I said; 'leave the horse here, Tucker, and help me into the saddle again.'"

"Tucker gazed at me in astonishment, but did as he was bid."

"'I am going to Culverton,' I said, shortly, taking up the reins."

"'To Culverton! At this hour, and in this weather!' said Tucker, in tones of alarm. 'Stay at any rate till you have had a night's rest, for you need it, master, and till I can put up what you need for the journey.'"

"'Let go my horse, man!' I cried, excitedly, setting spurs to the animal and abruptly ending the honest fellow's remonstrance."

"The thought of my father lying ill, dying perhaps, and me here revelling in Ogilby, made it impossible for me to contemplate a moment's delay, even so much as to change my gay attire or provide myself with necessaries for the journey. Culverton was thirty miles distant. I had a good horse, and with all my dissipation I was capable of a fair share of endurance. I therefore yielded to my impulse, and halting only to leave word with a comrade whom I met to explain my absence to the colonel, I dashed off into the night on my way to Culverton.

"What were my thoughts during those first few hours I need hardly tell you. I hope and trust none of you will ever be tortured by the self- reproach of which I was then the victim."

"For some distance out of Ogilby the roads were pretty good, and I made tolerable progress; so that when morning broke about seven I was at least a dozen miles on my journey. I could scarcely brook the delay of a few minutes at the first village to rest my horse and swallow a hurried breakfast; but I knew that for the rest of the way accommodation, either for man or beast, was very limited, and, therefore, prudence made the unwelcome delay a necessity."

"Once more in the saddle I hoped to make up for lost time; but in this I was fated to be disappointed. For scarcely had I got beyond the village when the weather suddenly changed. The chill morning air freshened to a wind which brought snow with it, light at first, but increasing in heaviness as the day went on. The road rapidly became covered, and my horse, unable on the treacherous foothold to maintain the canter of the morning, was compelled to slacken into a trot.

"I was in no gear for weather like this, as you may suppose. I still wore the light festive attire of the previous night, covered only with my military cape, which I now drew more closely around me at every step. How I wished I had taken Tucker's prudent advice! But it was too late to help it now."

"What troubled me most was not the cold, or the driving snow in my face, but the slow pace at which progress was now possible. I had hoped to reach Culverton by noon, but by noon I had accomplished scarcely two- thirds of the distance, and every moment the difficulties of the way were increasing. My horse trudged on gallantly. The trot had long since given place to a walk, and the walk in turn often became a sheer struggle for progress through the drifts and obstacles of the uncertain road.

"As for me, I was nearly frozen in my saddle, and more than once was compelled to dismount and tramp along beside my horse in the deep snow in order to keep the blood going in my veins. And all the while the thought of my father lying there at Culverton, neglected perhaps, with no son at hand to tend him, drove me nearly frantic."

"The afternoon dragged on, and towards dark the snow ceased to fall. That was at least some comfort, for to battle through that storm in the dark would have been an impossibility. As it was, my good horse was even now ready to drop, and I was in little better plight. If either of us failed it meant an entire night in the snow, and that would be little

Talbot Baines Reed

short of certain death. It was a dreary prospect.

"However, as I say, the snow ceased to fall, and towards night the sky overhead began to clear, until presently the moon shone out and lit up the wintry scene. But for this light we might have lost our way hopelessly, for the road lay over a heath, which being all covered in snow, we had only the wayside posts to direct us and keep us on the beaten track."

"It must have been near eight o'clock, sixteen hours since I had left the assembly at Ogilby, when I caught sight in the moonlight of a small cottage a little way removed from the road on our right. The sight of this, the first habitation we had passed for hours, was welcome indeed. I could scarcely stand with hunger, fatigue, and cold, and my brave horse was stumbling at every step. Our only chance of reaching Culverton that night was in seeking such rest and refreshment as this place might afford, and I therefore gladly turned aside and led my weary steed along the by-path that led up to it."

"It was a small tumbledown cottage, or rather barn, and my fond hopes as to fire and refreshment were dashed at once. It was empty. The broken door stood ajar, the roof was nearly fallen in, and everything within and without testified that for weeks at any rate it had been deserted. Still it had walls and a roof, and so if we were not to have board we might at least for an hour or so help ourselves to lodgings.

"I led my horse in, and after much groping about was delighted to discover in one corner of the hovel a sort of stall, which had evidently at one time or other been occupied by a cow. The ground was still strewn with a little old and very vile straw, which, however, was an unexpected luxury to us both, and a mere mouthful of stale hay remained in the trough. To these desirable quarters I conducted my faithful companion, who without ceremony devoured the hay, and then, too exhausted to stand, dropped into a recumbent posture, and lay stretched on his side on the straw. I quickly followed his example, creeping as close to his side as I could for the sake of the warmth, and thus we lay in the dark, resting as we had never rested before after our day's work.

"My own fear was lest I should fall asleep. In spite of my anxiety about my father, and my bitter reproaches against myself, I felt a stupor come over me which it was almost more than human nature to resist. Once or twice I dozed off for a moment, and then woke by an effort, each time more painful, until I was tempted at last to give in and resist no longer, whatever it cost.

"I had just come to this resolve when I became suddenly aware of the sound of voices in the cottage. Whoever they belonged to, I felt sure they must have entered after me, for I had explored every corner of the place when I took possession. They had probably entered during one of my fits of drowsiness."

My first impulse was to discover myself to the new comers, and see if they could help me and my horse in our distress. But on second thoughts I decided to remain where I was until I could ascertain at least who the intruders were, and if they had any better right in the cottage than I had. I was wide awake now, and raising myself noiselessly from my horse's side, I crawled to the side of the stall and peered over.

"By the uncertain light of a small fire of sticks which they had made, I saw two men sitting on the floor regaling themselves with bread and meat and the contents of a bottle. The sight of these good things made me still more inclined to disclose my presence, but prudence again forbade; besides which there was something strange about the look of the men, and the place where they were, which excited my curiosity."

"For a long time they continued their meal in silence. It went to my heart to see the victuals disappearing at such a rate, as you may suppose."

"At length, when, for the present at any rate, their appetites seemed to be appeased, they began to talk once more."

"'You're sure there's no mistake this time?' said one."

"'I have his own word for it,' replied the other. 'I tell you, Tom, he's planned it all out like Bonaparte himself.'"

"'All I can say is,' said he who was called Tom, 'I hope something will come of it, for I'm sick of all this doing nothing.'"

"'You may be sure something will come of this,' replied the other; 'and it will be something worth the while too, unless I'm mistaken, for the old gentleman is very rich; see here,' said he, producing some papers from his pocket, 'this is what he says.'"

"He began to read a letter, and you may fancy how I, listening behind the partition, started as I heard it."

"'Jack,' it said, 'I'm watched and can't come. You and Tom must do it without me. Be you know where by eight on Friday night, and I'll send one I can trust to show you the way and help you through with it. You may rely on him, though he's a queer dog. Here's a map of the grounds of Culverton, but you won't need it, for he I send knows the place well. The steward is on our side, and will leave the back door unlatched. The strong box stands in the study, the second door on the left after you pass the great clock. The old man lies ill, and only two maids are in the house besides. The young puppy is away at Ogilby. Bring what you get to the tower by the river on Saturday night. There are jewels in the desk in the old man's room. He cannot hurt—if he tries he must be quieted—you know how.'"

"I was so horrified that for a moment or two I scarcely knew whether I was awake or dreaming. My poor father, not only ill, but in peril of robbery, and perhaps murder! And I, what could I do? My impulse was to spring from my retreat and make one desperate effort to overpower the villains. But I was too weak to do it. Besides I was unarmed, whereas they had each his pistol. What could I do?

"The man who had read the letter carefully put it, along with the rough map of the Culverton grounds, into the fire, and the two sat and watched the papers as they burned."

"'He's a good man of business,' said Tom."

"'Middling,' replied the other; 'and if he—'"

"At that moment my horse gave a sudden start in his sleep. The quick ears of the two villains instantly caught the sound."

"'Hullo!' said one in a whisper, 'what was that?'"

"'Hist!' said the other, holding up his hand, 'strike a light, Tom.'"

"While Tom obeyed I softly dropped on my hands and knees and crawled back to my old place beside the horse, where I lay motionless, and to all appearance in a profound sleep."

"'I'm sure I heard something,' said Tom, holding up the lantern. From where they were they could see nothing but the side of the stall. They therefore crept round stealthily; and as I lay I saw the light suddenly turn on the horse."

"'A nag, as I'm a Dutchman, and saddled too!' exclaimed Tom."

"'If that's so, the rider's not far off,' said the other, grimly, taking the lantern and advancing."

"It was all I could do to lie motionless, breathing heavily, as the light fell full on my face."

"'Ah! found him!' was the exclamation, as both rushed towards me."

"I heard the cocking of a pistol close beside me, and was conscious of a rude plucking at my arm."

"'Come, get up there! What do you do here? Get up, do you hear?'"

"I had one hope left, and it was a desperate one."

"I roused myself slowly, and with many feints, from my mock slumber, and rubbed my eyes and yawned, and stared first at one, then the other."

"'Get up,' again cried the men, still pulling my arm roughly, 'and say what you're doing here.'"

"'Doing here?' I drawled as unconcernedly as I could, stretching myself at the same time, 'That's a pretty question to ask me. What were *you* doing not to be here at eight o'clock, I'd like to know?'"

"The men let go my arms, and looked at me in bewilderment."

"'Why,' said one, 'are you—'"

"'There,' said I, 'we don't mention names in our trade. You'll learn that when you grow older, and you'll learn to be punctual too,' I added, testily."

"The men looked half abashed."

"'We were here at eight,' they said."

"'No, you were not. I was here at eight to the minute, and I had time to fall asleep, as you see, before you came. But never mind that. You know what business is on foot, I suppose?'"

"'Yes, I had it all from—'"

"'Hush! no names, you dolt; what did I tell you before?'"

"The men were perfectly sheepish now, and I began to breathe again. It was well I had been described in the letter as a 'queer dog,' for it is an easy part to act, even to save one's own life. Besides, this would account sufficiently well for my unbusinesslike attire."

"My great fear was lest the real person referred to in the letter should arrive on the scene before I had quitted it. I therefore ordered an immediate departure."

"'We've lost an hour already with your dilatoriness,' I growled; 'don't let us lose any more. As it is, it is a chance if we reach Culverton before morning. Come, lead out my horse, and bring what food you have with you, for I'm starving.'"

"Before five minutes had passed we were safe out of the cottage and in the high-road—I, mounted on my faithful and partly refreshed horse, eating ravenously of the scraps of bread and meat my companions had left, while they trudged along in the snow one on either side."

"In this manner we progressed for an hour or so in silence, until about one o'clock there appeared on the side of a distant hill a twinkling light. I knew it at once. It had guided me home often and often before now, and it was doing so again. But in what strange company!"

"'That's Culverton, on the hill there,' said I."

"The men, who were nearly dead beat with their tramp through the deep snow, said nothing, but plodded on doggedly. It was nearly an hour more before we reached the outskirts of the estate, and by this time so exhausted were they that when I cried a halt they fairly sat down in the snow."

"I was strongly tempted to leave them there; but a desire to bring them to condign punishment prevented me. They were armed, and I was not. Besides, the reference in the letter to my father's steward made me anxious to sift the matter to the bottom."

"'Come, come,' said I, 'at that rate you'll never see the strong box. Get up, men!'"

"They struggled to their feet. Had they been anything but the villains they were I could have pitied them, they looked so miserable."

"'Hold my horse,' said I, dismounting, 'while I go and reconnoitre. I know every inch of the ground. Keep in the dark, whatever you do, under the hedge there. So. Are you loaded?'"

"'I am,' said Tom, sullenly taking out his pistol."

"'So am I,' said the other."

"'Give me one of the pistols,' I said, as coolly as I could. 'You won't want both here, and I may want one.'"

"Tom handed me his."

"'Now keep a look-out here, and when you hear me whistle over the wall, come sharp, mind!'"

"So saying, I left them, and went on towards the house."

"Except in my father's room no lights were burning, and I began to hope that what the letter had said about the steward might after all prove to be false. I went quietly up to the back door and turned the handle. It was open. The story was true, then, and in my rage and indignation I could hardly contain myself to act my part any longer. However, I made a desperate effort.

"Holding the door slightly open I whistled softly. There was no answer. I whistled again louder. This time there was a sound of some one moving, and the faint nicker of a candle, and presently I heard a voice whisper—

"'Is it all right?'"

"'All right,' I whispered back. 'And you, steward?'"

"'Yes. All ready. Come in.'"

"I entered. My hat was over my eyes, and in the faint candle-light the false servant did not know me. I followed him to his room."

"'You're late,' he said, reaching down some keys from a nail. 'Where are the rest?'"

"'Outside,' I replied in a low whisper."

"But, low as it was, the voice was not disguised enough to escape the quick ear of the steward. He turned sharply round and looked at me, while I at the same moment, throwing off my cap, sprang towards him and presented my pistol."

"He was too stunned and terrified to do anything but drop on his knees and utter incoherent entreaties and ejaculations for pity."

"'How is my father?' I inquired, not heeding his entreaties, and pointing the pistol still at his head."

"'Better,' he faltered—'much better. Oh, Master—'"

"'Come with me,' I replied, turning to the door."

"He accompanied me like a lamb. Had my father been worse I had intended to lock him up a prisoner in his own room. As it was, I took him silently and stealthily through the village and delivered him up then and there into the hands of the watch."

"This villain secured, it only remained to make sure of the other two. And this, as it happened, was a very easy task. For both, exhausted by their long, forced march and utterly benumbed by the cold, had fallen into a drowsy stupor under the hedge where they had been left, crouching beside my faithful steed for warmth. In this state it was simple work to secure them and march them off to custody, where at any rate they were not less comfortable for a time than they had been.

"A further visit next morning to the 'tower by the river,' which was well known to the watch as a rendezvous of thieves, served to secure the rest of the conspirators: and the law of the land shortly afterwards put it out of their power one and all to practise their wicked craft again."

"As for me, that night taught me a lesson or two that I've not forgotten to this day, and which in my turn I've tried to teach to some of you here. I went back to Ogilby a wiser man than I had left it, and, thank God, a better one."

"And what did the poor horse do?" asked the youngest of the Culvertons.

"Why, he carried me back as merrily as if he'd never seen snow in all his life."

CHAPTER THIRTEEN

OUR NOVEL

A SUMMER HOLIDAY ACHIEVEMENT

SUB-CHAPTER I

THE PLOT

It was a bold undertaking, no doubt, at our tender age, to propose to take the world by storm. But others had done it before us.

We had read our *Wonderful Boys* and our *Boyhood of Great Men* carefully and critically. We had seen that Mozart had composed music at six, and written it down very untidily too; we had seen that Marlborough had, by sheer cheek, been made an officer at about our age; that David Wilkie, one of the dullest of boys, had painted pictures while at school; that Scott, a notorious blockhead, had written poetry at thirteen; and that James Watt, at the same age, with very little education, had pondered over the spout of a tea-kettle.

All this we had seen, and been very greatly impressed, for surely, if some of these very ordinary boys had succeeded in startling their generation, it would be strange, if we two—Sydney Sproutels and Harry Hullock, who had just carried off the English composition prize at Denhamby—couldn't write something between us that would make the world "sit up."

That English composition prize had really been a great feather in our caps. It was the first thing of the kind we had done—not the first English composition, but the first sustained literary effort—and it had opened our eyes to the genius that burned within us.

The exercise had been to expand the following brief anecdote into an interesting narrative which should occupy two pages of Denhamby paper with twenty lines in a page:—

"Orpheus, son of Oeagrus and Calliope, having lost his wife, Eurydice, followed her to Hades, where, by the charm of his music, he received permission to conduct her back to earth, on condition that he should not look behind him during the journey. This condition he broke before Eurydice had quite reached earth, and she was in consequence snatched back into Hades."

I need not say that two pages of Denhamby paper were all too short to express all we had to say on this delightful subject. I, being by nature a poet, could have used all my space in describing the beauties of the spring morning on which Orpheus made his unusual expedition; while Hullock, whose genius was of a more practical order, confided to me afterwards that if he had had room he had intended to introduce a stirring conversation between the widower and his wife's ghost, in which the latter would make certain very stringent conditions before consenting to return once more to household duties.

Talbot Baines Reed

However, by dint of severe self-denial, we both managed to restrain our muses to the forty lines prescribed, and sent in our compositions with quite a feeling of envy for the examiner who would have to read them.

When the results were announced, the doctor publicly stated that "though many of the compositions were meritorious, yet, on the whole, those of Sproutels and Hullock showed most originality, and, indeed, gave considerable promise. The prize would be shared between them."

Of course, after that, all question as to our calling in life was at an end, and the sooner we "fleshed" our pens before the world the better. So it was arranged that Hullock was to get his father and mother to invite me for the midsummer holidays, and that before Denhamby saw us again, "Our Novel" should be started.

The Hullock family, it is necessary to say here, consisted of my partner, his two parents, a maiden aunt, and a sister. Mr Hullock, a good and worthy little man, who had not had all the advantages of education which his son possessed, was a retired coal merchant, spending the afternoon of his days at Saint Leonards.

His wife, as kind and motherly as she was tall and portly, treated me like her own son from the moment I entered her house.

And with her to look after me, and Alice to fall in love with, and Harry to collaborate with, I was about as comfortable as a restless genius could be—that is, I should have been so had it not been for the damp and frigid influence of Aunt Sarah, who sympathised neither with genius nor youth, and certainly not with the two in combination. Twenty times a day she grieved me by calling me "silly little boy," and twenty times a day she exasperated me by reminding Harry, and, through him, me, that "little boys should be seen and not heard."

However, we decided to ignore this uncongenial influence, and bury our sorrows in "Our Novel."

"Tell you what," said Harry, as we walked on the pier the first evening, "we ought to look sharp and get our plot."

"Wouldn't it be better to settle on the characters and get the plot afterwards?"

"All serene!" said Harry; "can you suggest any one for a hero?"

Harry said this in a half significant, half off-hand manner, which made it evident to me he expected I should at once nominate him.

But, in my judgment, Harry hardly possessed all the qualifications necessary for the hero of our novel. So I replied, half significantly, half off-handedly too—

"Hadn't *you* better think of some one?"

Here we were in a fix at the very start. For Harry insisted he would much rather that I should select, and I was equally anxious for him to do it.

At length we compromised the matter and decided we should make the hero a mixture of two fellows—the fellow Harry liked best and the fellow I liked best.

After this amicable arrangement it was comparatively clear sailing. We had not to look far for the heroine, and it occurred to both of us that it would be original as well as pleasant to make the villain a female and middle-aged. As for minor characters, we were able to draw on our acquaintance at Denhamby to supply them, and, failing that, Harry was magnanimous enough to offer his father and mother as "not bad for some of the side plots."

We had got our characters. That one walk on the pier settled them all. We also stopped a bit to watch the people, we entered into conversation with a sailor (who turned out to be deaf), and insinuated ourselves into the front of a street row, all with a view to reproducing our observations on life into "Our Novel."

The street row indeed furnished an inspiration for our plot. It was the arrest of a make-believe Italian female organ-grinder, whose offence appeared to be that she was carrying about in a cradle attached to the organ an infant that did not belong to her. And as the infant brought her in much more money than her music did, she protested in very strong English against having it removed.

With the quickness of genius we saw in this incident the pivot on which our novel should be made to turn.

The baby was the heroine, the organ-grinder the villain who had stolen her from her high-born station in life. Two of the characters fitted at a blow! We had even got the high-born parents ready if required, and when sixteen years later the little truant was to discover her noble station, we had our hero ready to take her home!

Between the pier-gate and Warrior Square we had the whole story worked out.

"What has kept you little boys out so late?" asked a voice as we entered Mr Hullock's hall. "It's not right. You should have been in bed by eight."

It was Aunt Sarah! and we secretly condemned her on the spot to a public execution in our last chapter.

As we undressed that evening another point was cleared up.

"We can't keep the hero hanging about sixteen years before we bring him in," said Harry.

"Humph," I observed, "unless we said 'sixteen years passed' at the end of the first chapter, and then we might get him in in the second."

"It strikes me," said Harry dubiously, "he ought to be in it all through. What do you say to making him another stolen baby belonging to another organ? Just as likely to have two stolen as one."

It did occur to me that if it came to that, all the characters in the story might begin life in this romantic way. However, there seemed no objection to starting the hero in an organ-grinder's cradle, and we closed with the suggestion at once and got into bed.

I woke very early. I had the hero on my mind. I wanted him to be a good one after the best model, and I could not help thinking that the Harry in him ought not to be overdone. Besides, if he was to make himself pleasant to the heroine, the less he was like Harry and the more he was like Harry's chief friend the better. For sisters in fiction never make much of their brothers, but they often make a lot of their brothers' friends.

I nudged Harry with my elbow, in order to represent the case

Talbot Baines Reed

to him from this point of view. I did it delicately and in a most conciliatory manner.

"I was thinking, old man, as Alice is the heroine and you're her brother, I might—don't you know—perhaps you'd like if—well, what I mean to say is, perhaps I'd better do the gush, when it comes to that."

Happily Harry was scarcely awake, and did not take in all my meaning.

"All serene," said he, "we'll have as little of that as we can."

"I mean I think you'd do the parts about the villain and that sort of thing better—don't you?"

But as Harry was asleep again I had to take silence for consent.

The day that followed was an anxious one. It is easy enough to get your characters, but it is awful having to fix their names. And it is simple work getting a plot, compared with the agony of dividing it up into forty chapters!

This was the task before us to-day, and we retired as before to the pier-head with pencils and paper, in order to do it beyond the sound of Aunt Sarah's voice.

We endured agonies over the names. The hero's name should naturally have been a judicious combination of the names of the two fellows we had in our minds' eyes. But neither "Sydrey Sproutock" nor "Hardney Hulltels" exactly pleased us. Finally we decided to call him Henry Sydney, and, strange to say, it occurred to me it would be best as a rule to speak of him by his surname, while Harry was equally strong about calling him by his Christian name. At last we agreed that when we, the authors, spoke of him it should be as Sydney, and that when the heroine or any one else mentioned his name it should be as Henry—Harry explaining that "as they're to be kids together there won't be anything strange in her calling him by his Christian name." The heroine, after much searching of heart, we christened Alicia Dearlove, and the villain Sarah Vixen.

The other names we made up from a local directory which we were lucky enough to stumble across in the pavilion.

Then came the formidable work of slicing up our novel into forty pieces. We wrote the figures down the side of a long sheet of paper, and looked with something like dismay at the work we had set before us.

"Seems a lot of chapters," said Harry; "couldn't we make it thirty?"

"Wouldn't run to six shillings if we did," said I.

That settled it, and we set ourselves to fill up the blanks.

"Chapter the First," wrote I. "Theft of Alicia—Sorrow of her Parents—The Organ-grinder's Lodgings—Suspicions of the Police—The Hero in the Room underneath."

"Hold hard!" cried Harry; "that's too much for one chapter. We shall have to make that do for four of 'em, or else we shall run out in ten."

"How on earth can you make four chapters of that?" said I.

"Well, you can make 'Theft of Alicia' spin out into one."

"Oh, ah! Why, all there is to say is that Aunt Sarah—I mean

Mother Vixen—came across her in the square and collared her. However are you to make a dozen pages of that?"

"Oh," said Harry, "we shall have to make her call at public-houses on the way, and that sort of thing, and describe the scenery in the square, and have the nursemaid go off to see the militia band go by, and leave the baby on the seat. Bless you, it'll spread out!"

Harry seemed to know all about it.

So we went, on with our skeleton, trotting our little foundling round town on the organ, where she witnessed with infant eyes street rows, cricket matches, bicycle races, a murder or two, and such other little incidents of life which we deemed calculated to enliven our story.

About the twelfth chapter she and our hero had already exchanged tender passages.

In the twentieth chapter her real father and mother happen to see her in the street (she being then sixteen), and are immediately struck by her resemblance to their lost baby.

By chapter twenty-five our hero had saved the lives of his future mother and father-in-law, and had rescued the heroine, single-handed, from a Hatton Garden mob.

In the twenty-ninth chapter Aunt Sarah had committed her murder with every circumstance of brutality and unpleasantness, the victim being one of our schoolfellows whom we neither of us loved.

Then for a chapter or two there was some very active police play, interspersed with a few love scenes between the hero and heroine, who—though it never occurred to us at the time—must have enjoyed independent means, which made it quite unnecessary for them to follow the ordinary avocations of organ-grinders.

About the thirty-fifth chapter there was to be a sudden drawing-in of threads from all quarters.

Sub-Chapter thirty-sixth was to be devoted to Sarah in the condemned cell.

Thirty-seventh—Alicia discovers her name by seeing it marked on a pocket-handkerchief she had been using at the time she was stolen.

Sub-Chapter thirty-eighth—The hero discovers his name by being told it by a solicitor who has known all about it all the time.

Sub-Chapter thirty-ninth—All comes right; everybody goes back to their mothers and fathers, and a quiet wedding ensues.

Sub-Chapter forty—Execution of Sarah. Finis.

We were tired and hungry by the time our paper was full, but we were jubilant all the same.

"Stunning fine plot!" said Harry. "If we only work it out it ought to be as good as *Nicholas Nickleby*."

"Rather! By the way, we ought to have one or two funny chaps in it to work off some of our jokes. There's that one about the sculptor dying a horrid death, you know—because he makes faces and busts! I'd like to get that in somehow."

"All serene! That might come in in the last chapters. I've got the *Family Jest-Book* at home; we might pick a few things out of that, and then settle where they come in, and work in for them as we go on."

We accordingly made a judicious selection, and having marked the initials of the character who was to bring them in against each, and also the number of the chapter in which they were to "come on," we really felt as if everything was now ready for our venture.

We went to bed early, so as to get a good night and arise fresh to our work, not, however, before we had made an expedition to the stationer's and expended half a crown in manuscript paper, J and D pens, blotting- paper, blue-black ink, and forty small paper-fasteners.

These provided, and the servant being particularly charged to call us at five o'clock, we retired to rest, and slept with our "skeleton" under the pillow.

SUB-CHAPTER II

THE PLOT THICKENS

A grave question arose the moment we opened our eyes next morning. Who was to write the first chapter? A great deal depended on how it was done. The style of the first chapter would give tone to the whole novel, and, so to speak, show the way for all the other chapters.

"I thought," said Harry, in his suspicious off-hand way, "if you took the even numbers and I took the odd, that might do."

Might it? That would mean he would write Chapter One. I wanted to write Chapter One. On the other hand, it would mean I should have Chapter twelve, with the execution in it, which would suit me very well. I mentioned the fact, and could see that Harry had forgotten it, for he tried hard to back out of his arrangement.

"I think you'd do the first chapter best," said he. "There's some scenery in it, you know, and you're more of a dab at that than I am."

But my modesty preferred the even numbers, and our novel looked very like being water-logged before she had even been launched.

A compromise was, however, arrived at. As the question of style was very important, it was decided we should *both* write Chapter One, and then, after comparing the two attempts, arrange our further procedure accordingly.

So I with a J pen, and Harry with a D retired to opposite

corners of the room and plunged headlong into the "Theft of Alicia." It was a hard morning's work, and by the time the breakfast-bell rang we were both getting the steam up. The sight of Aunt Sarah brooding over the tea- tray had but one meaning for us, and Sister Alice's pretty face and soft voice spoke to me only of that baby I had left in my chapter lying on the seat in the square.

"Now, little boys, are you going to play on the beach to-day?" said the villain, as the meal concluded.

"No, aunt," said Harry. "Syd and I have got some work we are doing."

"What work?" demanded Aunt Sarah.

"English composition," said Harry boldly.

And under cover of this truthful announcement we escaped.

It was midday before I laid down my pen and gathered my scattered sheets together. Harry had been done before me, but he had only written eleven sheets, so our pace was about equal.

"Done?" said he, as I sat back in my chair.

"Yes; lock the door," said I.

I must beg the reader's pardon if I do not lay before them the whole of the two lucubrations. They must be content with a few impartially chosen selections.

My chapter began with a poetical description of London in early morning.

"London in the morning! What a scene! The whistle of the workmen's trains sounds, and the noise of vegetable carts going to Covent Garden Market, give the place an animated appearance. Very few people are awake, and those that are look sleepy.

"In such a scene as this a hideous-looking woman, about fifty years old, with a long nose and a shabby barrel-organ, wended her way from some of the slums near Farringdon Street Station in the direction of Euston Square."

"It was not a very pretty walk. There were no birds twittering in the trees, or cuckoos. You could not hear the gentle roar of the ocean, and what flowers there were, were in pots on the window-sills."

"The ugly woman chose the road where there were most public-houses, and I am sorry to say that any one who had walked close beside her would have heard her talking to herself in very bad language."

Here followed the description of a few of the public-houses and their natural beauties, and my narrative proceeded—

"In this way the wicked woman reached Euston Square. She was greatly intoxicated, and not able to play the tunes on her organ correctly. Nobody gave her anything, which was not surprising, and the police moved her on all round the square.

"At last it was plain she would have to do something to get some money."

"After thinking over all the different things, she thought she would steal a baby and get money that way. So, seeing a baby lying on a seat close by, whose nurse had gone off to see a militia band marching towards Gower Street, she stole it and went off as fast as she could.

"There was a cradle hanging on to the organ, and when people saw the baby in it the wicked woman got as much money as she liked."

"My reader will have guessed by this time that the baby, which was of the feminine gender, is the heroine."

"She was really high-born."

"Her father was a retired coal merchant. He was a very little man and dropped his h's.

"Her mother was what the vulgar would call a 'whopper.' Let not the reader think she whopped her baby or her husband. On the contrary, she was kind, but big."

"They lived at Highbury, and the nurse always took the baby out for walks before breakfast."

It was at this point that it had suddenly flashed across me that I had left out the joke allotted to Chapter One, and as the narrative was well advanced, I ought to work up for it without delay. So I proceeded.

"We left Alicia, for that was the name of our heroine, being wheeled back on the organ to Hatton Garden. It was an unpleasant journey. The bad woman called at a lot more public-houses, and left Alicia and the organ outside in the rain."

"It was a wonder Alicia was not stolen again. She began to cry. People who came by couldn't make out what it was, for she was hidden under the quilt, and some thought instead of an organ it must have been some strange animal."

"An organ that cried like a child would be a very queer animal, nearly as queer as an author whose tale comes out of his head; and some of the people said so."

I was hot and tired by the time I had worked off this piece of humour, and began to wish I saw my way to the end of my twelve sheets. Two more I occupied with a picture of the organ-grinder's quarters in Hatton Garden, and concluded with the following poetical passage:—

"Little thought the wicked Vixen as she huddled her stolen infant into a damp corner of the filthy room, how much would happen before Alicia and her poor parents next met."

"We know very little of what is going to happen, and perhaps it is a good job. At any rate it was a good job for Alicia as she lay fast asleep."

"The world is all before the little baby—It doesn't know what's all in store for it—If it did know, it seems to me that maybe it wouldn't like the prospect—not a bit."

"End of Chapter One."

Harry looked a little uncomfortable as I finished reading my chapter aloud. I concluded he felt rather out of it, and I was not surprised. For on the whole it read well, and in some respects I flattered myself it had rather a pull on *Nicholas Nickleby.*

Harry wisely reserved his criticisms until he had read his own chapter, which I awaited with a smile of brotherly resignation.

"You know," explained he, before he began, "I tried to get more incident than you, that's why I left out the scenery."

Aha! my scenery had fetched him, then! I wondered what his incident would be like.

"Fire away!" said I.

"Her name was Sarah Vixen—[I'm beginning now]—Her name was Sarah Vixen. She was a horrid old maid. One morning she went and played her organ in Euston Square. She played 'Wait till the clouds roll by,' and 'Sweethearts' waltz', and the 'Marseillaise,' one after the other, after which she paused and watched a tennis match which was going on in the square.

"It was a four-handed match between two rather good-looking boys who wore red and green ribbons on their straws—[those were the Denhamby colours]—and two big London fellows. The schoolboys won the toss, and the fair one served first. He put in a very hot service just over the net, which broke sharp as it fell, and bothered the Londoners completely. The dark hand-in played close up to the net, and was very neat in the way he picked up balls and smashed them over."

Harry paused and looked doubtfully at me for a moment, and then went on.

"The schoolboys pulled off the first three games, and then the Londoners scored a game, owing to the wind. A large crowd collected to see the match, and shouts of 'Well put over!' greeted the schoolboys on every hand. The Londoners didn't score another game in the first set, and scored nothing in the second."

"The crowd became thicker and thicker every moment. In the last game the fair schoolboy spun a ball into the far left-hand corner, which the Londoner could not reach, and the match ended in a glorious victory for the two schoolboys, who, apparently unaware of the cheers of the crowd, walked home arm-in-arm as if nothing had happened."

"On their way they met a runaway horse, and loud cries of 'Take care!' 'Get out of the way!' met them on all sides. A nursemaid was wheeling a child across the road at that moment, and quick as thought the fair boy sprang at the horse and brought him to a standstill just in time. The crowd seeing it, rushed with a great cheer to the young hero, but he seeing it, took his friend's arm and walked on as if nothing had happened.

"'What are you so pale for?' asked his friend."

"'Oh, nothing very much. I have broken my arm; but it really doesn't matter much.'"

"While he spoke he fainted, and if it had not been for his friend, might have fallen."

"Meanwhile the baby, left to herself in the perambulator in the middle of the road, began to cry, which attracted the notice of Vixen, who, seeing she was a nice child, went and lifted her out of her perambulator, and put her in her cradle on her organ while nobody was looking, and took her to her home."

"'Whose home?' I asked."

Harry did not condescend to notice this interruption. He may have guessed I was jealous. All that about the heroic fair boy had been taking an unfair advantage of me, and I think he knew it. For I was of a dark complexion! His narrative went on to describe a fight in the organ-grinder's lodgings, and a burglary, followed by a fire at the residence of the parents of the lost child. As a matter of course, the fair boy with his broken arm turned up on the fire-engine, and brought most of the family down the escape with his sound arm. Then by a sudden transition the scene changed back to the organ-grinder's "cottage," on the ground floor of which in another cradle slept another infant, a boy, fair, of course, and beautifully made, showing great promise of physical force and heroism of disposition.

"He was older than Alicia, and could speak a little. There was no one in the room, and as he sat up in his cradle he felt very sad. Presently two young organ-grinders came into the room. One was dark and vicious, the other was fair [of course] and had a pleasant expression. They took no notice of the baby, but sat and smoked and asked riddles of one another. The fair one [of course!] was far the cleverer of the two, and caused much laughter by his wit.

"'Can you tell me,' said he, in a pleasant silvery voice very unlike an organ-grinder, 'why an author is a queer animal?'"

"'Give it hup,' said the vulgar one, who always put his 'h's' wrong."

"'Because his tale comes out of his head!'"

"It was long before the vulgar one saw it, and then he laughed so much that the baby began to cry, and they had to go into the next room for fear of disturbing it. Having left the door open, the fair baby got out of its cradle, and, being old enough to walk, went quietly upstairs, and there what should he see in a cradle in the room above but Alicia! This was the first time the two met. They did not say much, but Cupid's arrow went through them both from that minute. That's all," said Harry."

There was a silence, which at last I broke.

"And which chapter do you think we'd better put in?"

"That's just what I was going to ask you," said Harry.

"You see," said I cautiously, "you've got rather a lot about that fair chap in yours, and he's not in the plot."

"Oh, he turns out somebody," said Harry.

"Who?"

"I don't know yet."

"He's not the hero, of course?" said I decisively; "he's to be a mixture of both."

"Oh, of course," said Harry. "But, I say, don't you think there's rather too much about scenery in yours? There's very little of that in *Nicholas Nickleby*, or poetry either."

"No; that struck me as one of the weak points of *Nicholas Nickleby*," said I.

"I thought it was settled the hero was to be in it from the first?" said Harry, falling back on another line of defence.

"So he is. I shall say in the next chapter that he was in the room underneath all the time," said I, rather testily.

"Oh, well," said Harry, "of course if you think yours is the best, you'd better stick it in. I'm out of it, if you're going in for poetry."

"You're not obliged to do any poetry," said I. "Thanks. I

shouldn't try unless I was sure of writing something that wasn't doggerel," said Harry. This was hitting me on a tender point. "Look here," said I, starting up, "do you mean to tell me I write doggerel?"

"I didn't say so."

"You meant it. I'd sooner write doggerel than stuff I'd be ashamed to read in a 'penny dreadful.' Call yourself a fair boy!"

Alas for our novel! We spent half an hour that evening in anything but a literary competition.

Aunt Sarah remarked on Harry's black eye and my one-sided countenance at breakfast next morning, and inquired artlessly if *English composition* had caused them. We truly answered, "Yes."

Our friendship was quickly restored; but our poor novel, after that one evening, has never lifted up its head again. We have sometimes vaguely talked of finishing it, but we have been careful to avoid all discussion of details, still less all reference to Chapter One. In fact, we have come to the conclusion that it is better not to startle the world at too early an age. If you do, you are expected to keep it up, and that interferes with your enjoyment of life.

When our Novel does come out, well, we think Conan Doyle, Wells, and those other fellows will sit up.

CHAPTER FOURTEEN

PREFACE

OUR OWN PENNY-DREADFUL

I am always coming across old manuscripts. I am not sure of the date of the following, but I fancy it must have been written for a prize, which, strange to say, it failed to secure. The only conditions were that the story should have lots of "go" in it, that the incidents should be natural, the tone elevating, and the characters carefully studied.

I ask any of my readers if this does not fulfil all these conditions? I know when it was returned to me as "not quite the style we care about," I was extremely angry, and replied that I should very much like to see what style they did care about, if not this. They had not the common politeness to reply!

Another publisher to whom I submitted it actually wrote back that he was not in the habit of publishing "penny dreadfuls." I was never so insulted in all my life!

However, as a specimen of the kind of story some boys read, and some editors do *not* publish, the reader shall have my "penny dreadful," and decide for himself whether it has not lots of "go," is not strictly true to nature, elevating in tone, and carefully studied. If it is not, then he had better not read it!

The Plaster Cast; Or Septimus Minor's Million.

A Thrilling Story in Fifteen Chapters, by the Author of "Blugram Blunderbuss, or the Dog-Man."

SUB-CHAPTER I

THE MURDER!

The golden sun was plunging his magnificent head angrily into the sheen of the bronze Atlantic when Septimus Minor scaled the craggy path which leads from Crocusville to the towering cliff above.

The wind came and went in fitful gusts, which now and again carried Septimus off his feet, and sometimes lifted him a foot or two over the edge of the rugged cliff in time for another eddy to carry him back.

Nature this evening suited the gusty humour of Septimus Minor's breast.

"The crisis of my life approaches!" he said to himself, as a magnificent wave from below leapt eight hundred feet in the air, and fell, drenching him from head to foot. "I am fifteen years old next week, and something here,"—here he laid his right hand on his left side—"tells me I am a man."

As he spoke, another wave leapt skyward, and out of it emerged the form of a man.

"Yes!" cried Septimus. "Her father!"

Septimus was the youngest of seven children, most of whom were orphans. But we digress.

"Belay there—haul in your mainslacks, and splice your marline-spike. Where are you coming to?" cried Peeler, the coastguardsman—for such, we need hardly say, was the rank of the new arrival.

"How are you?" said Sep, in an off-hand way.

"Blooming," said the not altogether refined Peeler.

A gust of wind lifted them both up the twenty remaining yards of the cliff, and left them standing on a sheltered crag at the extreme brink.

"Spin us a yarn," said Sep.

The setting sun cast a lurid flash over the figures of that strangely assorted pair. The next moment it had set, and nothing was visible but the reflection of the end of Sep's cigar in the glass eye of his interlocutor.

Septimus Minor had lived in Crocusville ever since he could remember, and the coastguardsman some years longer. Hence Sep's request.

Mr Peeler was a fine specimen of his class. He wore a sou'wester and boots to match, and round his shoulders—

But why all this minute detail concerning one who is to disappear—if he had but known it!—before that howling night—

"Twas in '52 she grounded," said he, transferring something from his right cheek to his left. "Hang me on the Union Jack," (that was a nautical expression by which Peeler added solemnity to his statement) "if there was not exactly one million Spanish doubloons on board."

Sep whistled, but immediately checked himself, and sat down on the wind to hear the rest.

"Bust my buttons if mortal man knows where she lies!"

continued Peeler, "save and except yours 'umbly. Stand by, my shaver, and cast your cock- eye on this bit of rag."

And he produced from his pocket a greasy piece of parchment with a map upon it.

"There," said he, laying his broad thumb on a red cross somewhere in the West Pacific, "there she lies—full of gold, my boy. Shiver my jury- masts if she don't."

The wind on which Sep was sitting lifted him to his feet, as he grasped the map and gazed with quivering excitement on the mysterious red mark.

He laughed sardonically, and the perspiration stood in beads on his brow. Then, pushing Peeler over the cliff, he put the map in his pocket, and walked on whistling in the night air to the cottage.

Talbot Baines Reed

SUB-CHAPTER II

THE SMILE

"My own Velvetina!"

"Sep, my pet!"

"Can it really be?"

"Even so."

A silence, during which a pair of tangled eyelashes are dim with humid dew. Then—

"Did you meet daddy on the cliff, pet?"

He turned ashy white, even in the darkness, and recoiled several yards at the unexpected inquiry.

"Where?" at last he gasped, prevaricatingly.

"Then you saw him not!" cried she, "and he is out alone on this wild night; and only his thin socks on."

"Really?" replies Sep, "let me go and look for him."

He crushed her lily hand lovingly in his own and went. But he turned to the left at the end of the lane, and with scarcely half a dozen bounds reached the railway station, grasping the map and murmuring to himself, "My Velvy!" all the way.

Any one who could have seen that happy boy's face at the window of the second-class carriage, as the train steamed majestically out of the station, would scarcely have dreamed of the deep meaning concealed beneath that ingenuous smile.

Smile on, Septimus, yet beware! The sleuth-hound is already on the track!

SUB-CHAPTER III

THE SLEUTH-HOUND

Solomon Smellie, of Scotland Yard, had yet his way to make in the world. He was not exactly young, for time had already thinned the luxuriant growth of his hair, nor was he without encumbrance, for he had fifteen children. Yet he was an active and intelligent officer, and had once detected something—he forgot what. But that is not to the point.

What brought him, walking on this particular evening, to the foot of the beetling cliffs?

Ask the howling wind, which ever and anon flattened him against the chalk or drove him miles inland up some cavernous cave. Be that as it may, he walked.

"I wish I could detect something in all this," said he, pulling himself together, and glancing scornfully into the darkness.

As he did so, Captain Peeler's corpse alighted gracefully on the sand at his feet.

"Ah, ha!" said he, "this looks like business. Now let me think. How comes this here?"

There were no footsteps in the sand beside his own, therefore the miscreant or miscreants must have escaped in some other direction.

"Aha!" said he, presently looking up. "They may be up there."

And he leapt actively to the beetling summit.

"Better and better," said he, looking round him and observing a hoof mark in the yielding clay, of which he promptly took a plaster cast. "Another link, ha, ha! the murderer was a horseman!"

And he sat down and wrote a lucid report on the whole case for his sergeant.

Solomon Smellie was in luck assuredly! Scarcely had he concluded his literary labour, when, at a distance, he perceived a twinkling light.

"Ha, ha!" said he, "now see how the real artist in crime works. Yonder is a light. The murderer cannot have gone that way. Therefore he has gone this."

And he stepped into the railway station just as Sep's train steamed out.

"Too late, this time," muttered he, between his teeth. "But time will show—time will show!" Never did man speak a truer word!

SUB-CHAPTER IV

THE STOWAWAYS

The "Harnessed Mule" was a splendid vessel of a hundred and fifty tons; and as she sailed past the Nore like a floating queen flapping her white wings in the breeze, she reminded the beholders that England still rules the waves.

Her crew consisted of a skipper, four men, and a boy.

Was that all?

Who is this lurking figure in the forward hold, who, with a complacent smile on his lips, gazes on a crumpled map, and ever and anon sharpens a gimlet?

There is a stowaway on board the "Harnessed Mule."

One? There are two.

For in the stern hold lurks another figure, also smiling, as the wind plays through the thin hair on the top of his head, and mutters to himself—

"Ha! ha! Time will show."

Sail on, O "Harnessed Mule." You carry a weighty freight inside you. Who will reach the goal first?

SUB-CHAPTER V

THE WRECK OF THE "HARNESSED MULE"

Latitude 80 degrees 25 minutes, longitude 4 degrees 6 minutes—a hot, breathless day. The "Harnessed Mule" glides swiftly over the unruffled blue. The crew loll about, listening to the babbling of the boiling ocean, and now and then lazily extinguishing the flames which break up from the tropically heated planks. It is a typical Pacific day.

The stowaway in the forward hold lies prone, conning his map, and marking the gradual approach of the "Harnessed Mule" to the red cross marked there. Frequently he is compelled to raise himself into a sitting position to give vent to the merriment which possesses him.

"This is better than Latin prose," says he to himself. "How jolly I feel!"

Could he but have guessed that through an adjoining crack another figure was drinking in every word he uttered, and taking it down in official shorthand, he would have spoken in less audible tones!

Yes. The second stowaway is Solomon Smellie, of Scotland Yard, and he has the plaster cast in his pocket.

"This must be about the spot," says Sep, comparing his chart with the figures on the mariner's compass. "Here goes."

Two vigorous turns of the gimlet, and the "Harnessed Mule" rears on her beam ends, and, with one stupendous lurch, goes to the bottom.

Talbot Baines Reed

"That's all right," says Sep, as he hauls himself to the summit of a mountain of naked rock, which rises sheer out of the sea on all sides to a height of a thousand feet.

The words are scarcely out of his mouth when his face turns livid, and he trembles violently from head to foot, as he perceives standing before him Solomon Smellie, the detective of Scotland Yard.

SUB-CHAPTER VI

THE RENCONTRE

"This is an unexpected pleasure," says Solomon.

"Delighted, I'm sure," says Septimus, craftily.

Then they talk of the weather, eyeing one another like practised fencers in a death struggle.

"Ha! ha!" thinks Sep; "he has heard of the sunken doubloons."

"Ha! ha!" thinks Solomon. "If he only knew I had that plaster cast in my pocket!"

"Are you making a long stay here?" says the former naively.

"Depends," is the dark, laconic reply.

"Sorry I must leave you for a little," says Sep. "An appointment."

And he takes a magnificent header from the cliff into the very spot where the wrecked gold-ship lies buried.

When, after a couple of hours, he rose to the surface for breath, Sep was relieved to find himself alone.

"Peeler was right," said he to himself, flinging back the matted hair from his noble brow. "My fortune is made."

And he dived again.

In the damp cabin of the sunk ship stood the gaunt form of many a brave mariner, faithful to his post even in death. Seth gave them a passing glance, and shuddered a little as he met their glassy eyes. He was about to rise to the surface with the remainder of his booty, when the figure nearest the door fell against him.

Turning on him, a cold perspiration suffused our hero from head to foot, and his hair rose like porcupine quills on his head.

It was not a corpse, but Solomon Smellie, the detective of Scotland Yard.

Sep had barely time to close to the cabin door, and strike out with his precious bags for the surface. He felt he had had a narrow escape of detection, and that the sooner he sought a change of climate the better.

As for Solomon, it would have needed a strong door to keep him from his prey.

"Ha, ha!" said he, "the chain grows link by link. Two and two make four. Patience, Solomon, and you will be famous yet."

SUB-CHAPTER VII

THE FETE AND THE FRACAS

It was the most brilliant ball which had ever been given in the English capital.

The very waiters sparkled with diamonds!

The gorgeous suite of apartments, several miles in length, were ablaze with all that wealth and beauty in electric light could effect.

Coote and Tinney's band was in attendance.

Down the sparkling avenues of lustres whirled the revellers in all the ecstasy of the hilarious dance.

Peals of laughter and the rustling of fans combined to make the scene the most gorgeous ever witnessed in this or any other metropolis.

The host of the princely revel was a mysterious young foreign nobleman, known by the name of the Duc de Septimominorelli, and reputed to be the richest man in Europe.

What makes this evening's entertainment particularly brilliant is the fact that it is to be graced by the dazzling presence of the peerless Donna Velvetina Peeleretta, who, as every one knows, is shortly to wear the diamond tiara of the house of Septimominorelli.

In other words, she and the Duc are betrothed.

The festivities are at their height, and the Duc for the fifth time is leading his charming *fiancee* to the supper-room, when the venerable butler announces, in a voice that attracts universal attention, a new arrival.

"Monsieur le Marquis de Smellismelli!"

If possible the Marquis was more magnificently attired even than the Duc, and went through the salutation with the easy grace of a man who had often appeared in Court.

"Who is he?" asked every one.

"An old college friend," explained the Duc.

But his face was the colour of his handkerchief, and the place shook with the trembling of his limbs.

The marquis quickly made himself at home, and vied with his host in his eagerness to take the Donna Velvetina down to supper.

The Duc's face darkened visibly in proportion as that of his guest beamed; and to those who looked on, it was evident that a scene was imminent.

At length, when for the nineteenth time the lady accepted the arm of the gallant marquis, the Duc ground his teeth, and stepping up to his rival, pulled his nose.

The marquis in return flung the Duc the entire length of the apartments, and with folded arms calmly awaited the result.

"We fight, Monsieur le Marquis," ground out the smarting Duc.

"Rather!" replied the marquis, with a proud smile.

SUB-CHAPTER VIII

THE DUEL

It was a tragic end in that night's gay scene.

Guests whose carriages were not ordered till 4 a.m. stood shivering in the hall at 11 p.m.

Five hours to wait!

Meanwhile, on two special steamers the Duc de Septimominorelli and the Marquis de Smellismelli sought the shore of France.

On the lonely sands between Calais and Ushant the rivals stood face to face, at a hundred paces distance.

They had no seconds, so each loaded the other's weapon.

It could not have been the wind that made their knees tremble and their teeth chatter, for there was none. Neither could it have been the weight of the pistols which made their hands wave to and fro, for these were Boxer's eight-ounce Maxim Repeaters.

No; these two men were the subjects of deep physical emotion. The moment had come, and the Duc was about to drop his handkerchief, when the Marquis abruptly folded his arms and said, "Excuse me, we have met before, have we not? Ha, ha, Sep, my boy!"

At the sound of his voice, the so-called Duc flung his weapon two hundred yards in the air, and with the bound of a hunted tiger buried himself in the turmoil of the French capital.

There was no duel on those yellow sands after all.

SUB-CHAPTER IX

AFTERWARDS

The mysterious disappearance of the dazzling Duc de Septimominorelli created a profound impression throughout civilised Europe. The Donna Velvetina Peeleretta was inconsolable.

After a while she, too, went abroad.

SUB-CHAPTER X

THE SLEUTH-HOUND AGAIN

Many, many years flew past.

Solomon Smellie's youngest son had been twice Lord Mayor of London, and all London had forgotten the Duc de Septimominorelli and the peerless Donna Velvetina Peeleretta.

All? No, there was one exception.

An aged man in a back room of the Mansion House sometimes produced a plaster cast from the recesses of his pocket, and muttered to himself—

"A time will come—aha!"

SUB-CHAPTER XI

THE DESERT JOURNEY

A lonely traveller traversed the sandy desert wastes of Central Africa. He was ill-accoutred for so trying a journey, having only a cane to protect himself from the wild beasts, and patent-leather shoes on his feet. No one knew his name; and what made him more mysterious was that, although he spoke English, he paid for everything in Spanish doubloons half a century old!

What could his errand be, amid the typhoons and siroccos of that desolate continent?

For six weeks he had not moistened his parched lips with so much as a drop of water! And his only food had been dried elephant!

Yet he kept his eyes fixed on the mountain range twelve hundred leagues ahead of him; and as each day brought him fifty miles nearer (for he was evidently a practised walker), he murmured to himself, "I come, Velvetina!" and thought nothing of the fatigue.

The man's shoes were unequal to his spirit, and within a hundred miles of his goal he sunk crippled to the ground. The blinding sand swept over him in mountains, and the tropical sun made the end of the cane he carried red-hot.

Any other man in such a condition would have succumbed. Not so our mysterious traveller.

If he could not walk, he could roll. And he rolled.

SUB-CHAPTER XII

THREE CLOUDS ON THE HORIZON

On the summit of the topmost of those gigantic mountains, the peak of which is lost high in the depths of the cloudless sky, a female stands, and gazes southward.

Her fair form is mysteriously draped in white, and the parasol with which she shuts out the scorching sun from her face effectually conceals her features.

"He cometh—he cometh not," says she, weeping.

At length, in the remote horizon of the limitless desert, there arises a little cloud of dust.

Is it a panther seeking its prey? or a newspaper buffeted by the wind? or the mirage of the desert?

It is the revolving form of a rolling body; and as she discovers it she trembles like an aspen leaf.

"He comes," mutters she.

Another cloud of dust; not in the south, but in the east.

Can it be an optical delusion, or another revolving figure? Ever and anon the sun gleams on something bright, which looks like the end of a cane.

A sickening sensation comes over the watcher.

"They both come!" says she; and turns her eyes northward.

What! Is it another optical delusion, or is this yet one more cloud in the north, which, as it approaches, also takes the semblance of a revolving figure? Hot as the weather is, she shivers sensibly, and, closing her parasol, mutters, her lips as white as driven snow—

"They all come!"

Talbot Baines Reed

SUB-CHAPTER XIII

THE WATCHER ON THE CAIRN

Twenty-four hours of agonising suspense, and then the revolving figures reach the base of the mountain, and commence simultaneously to roll up the side.

The female figure on the top gives a despairing glance around her, and drops senseless on the cairn.

At length, as the sun is setting in the only unoccupied horizon, she starts, rigid and stiff, and listens.

On either side of her approaches a dull grinding noise, mingled with heavy snorting, and the low muttering of voices.

She dares not look: it is terrible enough to hear!

So evenly do they approach, that at the same instant they reached the summit.

Then she rises majestically to her full height, spreads her arms, and utters a cry which is heard simultaneously at Cairo, at Zanzibar, and at Cape Town.

A terrible silence follows, broken only by the trembling of the mountain and the breathless panting of the three figures as each rears himself slowly to his feet.

The scene that followed may be more easily imagined than described.

SUB-CHAPTER XIV

ALL COMES OUT

It is time we went back to the scene on the cliff at Crocusville narrated in the opening chapter.

Peeler, the coastguardsman, after descending the cliff, resumed his ordinary avocations, and sent his daughter to a superior high school.

Hence her presence at the Duc's ball and on the desert mountain.

The Duc de Septimominorelli (for such was the mysterious traveller) recoiled several hundred yards on finding himself confronted not only by the aged father of his now middle-aged Velvetina, but by the form of his old opponent the Marquis de Smellismelli.

"Aha!" said the latter, producing his plaster cast. "How do you find yourself, Sep, my boy?"

"Hot," said Septimus, with characteristic coolness.

"Introduce me to the old gentleman," said the detective.

"Peeler," was the laconic reply.

It was Solomon's turn to turn inquiringly to the lady.

She only bowed.

"I wish very much I had known this before. I have wasted fifty years over you," said Solomon, in injured tones. "I must lose no more time if I am to detect anything. Good morning. Aha!

"Stay!" shouts Sep, in a voice of thunder. "It is I who have wasted fifty years running away from you. You owe me an apology, sirrah!"

The caitiff's face underwent a kaleidoscopic change as these terrible words rant? in his ears. With the bound of of a wounded antelope he sprang to the summit of the nearest mountain, and stood there with arms erect against the sky, like a statue of Ajax.

"He don't seem blooming, shiver my timbers if he do," said old Peeler.

"We shall not meet again," said Sep, grinding his teeth in his direction.

"Why should we be standing here in the sun?" said Velvetina. "Let us return to England."

They returned the same evening.

SUB-CHAPTER XV

OMNIA VINCIT AMOR

Septimus Minor and Velvetina Peeler were married quietly at the Crocusville Cathedral.

The bride was given away by her father, Captain Peeler, R.N.

The company was select and the presents were costly.

Amongst the latter none attracted more attention or curiosity than an excellent plaster cast of a horse's hoof, presented to the happy couple by the Marquis de Smellismelli and his grandson the Lord Mayor of London.

There were few knew its history; but it was eloquent in meaning for Mr and Mrs Septimus Minor, who have given it an honoured place on the mantelpiece of the second spare bedroom of their bijou residence in Pink Street.

Talbot Baines Reed

CHAPTER FIFTEEN

A QUEER PICNIC

SUB-CHAPTER I

A MYSTERIOUS MOUNTAIN

Magnus minor and my brother Joe were about as chummy as two fellows who had not a single taste in common could well be. Magnus, you know, was an athlete. At least, he was in the fourth eleven, and ran regularly in the quarter-mile open handicap. He got fifty yards the first year, and came in tenth; in the second year they gave him a hundred, and he came in eighteenth; in the third year they generously gave him a hundred and twenty yards, and he never came in at all, for some unexplained reason. After that he passed as an athlete, and considered himself an authority, especially at home, on all matters relating to sport. Joe, on the other hand, was a dreamy boy; he wrote poems, when he should have been construing Caesar, and gave several other indications that he was destined to a great career. He cared as little about sport as Magnus did about poetry. This probably was the reason the two were such chums. They never trod on one another's toes.

When they went for a walk, Joe usually dawdled along trying to think of rhymes for "nightingale," and "poppy," and "windmill," and the other beauties of Nature which met his eye or ear; while Magnus stopped behind to vault gates (which always caught his foot as he went over), and do "sprints" with wayside animals, in which the wayside animals usually managed to pull off the event. I'm not sure that they ever talked to one another, which again may have been a reason for their great friendship. If they did, nobody ever heard them; indeed, they never seemed to look at one another, or to be aware of one another's existence, which no doubt fully explains their mutual devotion.

The only real bond of sympathy that I can think of was that they were always going in for examinations together, and always getting plucked. Had the name of either ever appeared on a prize list, I am convinced there would have been a panic in the school. Even when they entered for the Wheeler Exhibition for boys under 15, Joe being on the day of examination 14 years 364 days, and Magnus being a week younger, no one supposed for a moment they had a chance against the fellows of eleven and twelve who went up against them; and no one was disappointed.

I asked Magnus afterwards how it was he came to grief.

"It was those beasts, the Greek gods. I'd like to kick them," said he.

By an odd coincidence I put the same question on the following day to my young brother.

"Eh?" said he, "what do you call them, you know, the thingamybobs that lived in Mount what's its name? I'm sick of 'em."

"Mount Olympus, you mean?"

"That's it—"

"Mount Olympus, Pack of Shrimpers."

This was a good specimen of my brother's poetic style!

I gathered from this that a new bond of sympathy had arisen between the two friends. They had both been ploughed in an unexpected paper on Greek Mythology, and were in consequence death on the divinities. I genuinely pitied the divinities!

Well—mind, as I wasn't in the affair, I can only relate it as I heard it—a very curious adventure happened to Magnus Minor and my young brother, shortly after this.

It was in the holidays, and we went, as usual, to Llandudno; and oddly enough, Magnus's people went there too. The two chums consequently had an opportunity of feeding the fires that consumed them, and of carrying on their feud with the Greek gods in boats and bathing machines, on the Great Orme's Head, and in the pier refreshment-room. Whenever I came across them they were still implacable; and once or twice I believe they actually spoke to one another on the subject, which shows how deeply they felt.

One day they made up their minds to do Snowdon, and with a respectable basket of provender, and an alpenstock apiece (on which the name of the mountain—in fact, several mountains, had already been cut), they started off by the train to Llanberis.

Magnus minor, being an athlete, occupied most of the journey in training himself on cold boiled eggs and damsons;

while Joe, being a poet, read somebody's "Half Holiday" in a corner.

At the place where the train stopped they got out, and wondered whether they had not already had enough of it. It was a grilling hot day. They hadn't an idea which was the way to Snowdon, and nobody seemed to know. A railway porter said "Second to the right"; but they could see he was humbugging. As if a mountain *could* be up a turning!

"Let's jack it up," said Magnus, who was feeling a little depressed after the damsons.

"Eh?" said Joe, "there's no train back to what's-his-name for two hours. What would it cost to cab it up?"

"Oh, pots," said Magnus. "I tell you what—we might have a go of ginger-beer somewhere, and see how we feel after that."

Whereupon in silence they found out the leading hotel or the place, and expended sixpence apiece on ginger-beer, at threepence a bottle.

Naturally they felt much refreshed after this, and, without condescending to further parley, decided to stroll on; only, as the porter had mentioned a turning to the right, they selected a turning to the left as decidedly more probable.

It may have been Snowdon, or it may not—in any case it was a hill, and a stiff one.

Magnus, the athlete, taking out his watch, said he meant to do it under twenty minutes, and begged Joe to time him.

Joe, the poet, agreed, and sat down on the shady side of a

rock with the watch in one hand, the "Half Holiday" in the other, and his share of the damsons in his mouth.

"How long have I been?" shouted the athlete, after stumbling up the slippery grass slope for about five minutes.

"Time's up!" shouted the poet.

Whereat Magnus, surprised at the rapid flight of the enemy, checked his upward career, and not only did that, but, assaying to take a seat on the grass, began to slide at a considerable pace, and in a sitting posture, downwards, until, in fact, he was providentially brought up short by the very rock under which his friend rested.

"*Facilis descensus Averni*," observed Joe, making a brilliant sally in a foreign tongue.

The remark was followed by instant gloom. It was too painfully suggestive of the heathen deities. Besides, Magnus had nearly smashed himself against the rock, and had to be brought round with more cold boiled eggs and damsons.

After this the ascent was resumed in a more rational way. They accomplished a quarter of a mile in the phenomenal time of two hours, during which period they sat down fourteen times, drank at twenty-one streams, fell on their noses about eighty times, and wished a hundred times they had never heard the name of Snowdon.

"I thought you said there was a 'thingamy' all the way up?" said Joe.

"So there is—we're on it," said Magnus minor.

"Oh," said Joe. He had previously had some misgivings that

he was growing shortsighted, but he was convinced of it now.

At the rate at which they were going there was every prospect of getting to the top of the first ridge about three o'clock on the following afternoon. But Magnus minor and my brother Joe were fellows who preferred doing a thing thoroughly—even though speed had to be sacrificed to the thoroughness.

So they pegged on, detesting this mountain as if it had been Olympus itself, and making a material difference in the level of the lakes below by the number of tributary streams they tried to drink up by the way.

At last they actually began to get up a bit.

"How far now?" said Joe, lying on his back with his coat off, his shirt- sleeves turned up, his collar off, and his braces slack.

"Just about there," said Magnus minor.

He spoke figuratively, of course. They were a quarter of the way up, perhaps.

"I don't believe this beast is what-you-may-call-him at all. It strikes me we ought to have turned to the—you know."

"It looks like him," said Magnus. "Anyhow, it'll do for him."

"I'd like to do for him," growled Joe.

They went on presently, in shocking tempers, both of them. They loathed that mountain, and yet neither liked to propose to go back. That is the way in which a good many mountains are climbed.

Magnus got riled with Joe for not giving in—he was the elder, and it was his business to begin. Joe, on the other hand, never thought so ill of Magnus as when he saw him pegging up twenty yards ahead, never giving him (Joe) time to catch up. He made faces at him behind his back, and tried to think of all the caddish things he had done since he came to the school. But it was no good. As sure as ever Joe tried artfully to cut a corner or "put it on" for a yard or two, Magnus, on ahead, cut a corner and put it on too.

When Magnus presently, having improved his lead, sat down to rest, Joe made sure he had caught his man at last. But— would you believe it?—just as he approached the place, with every show of friendship, announcing that he had something particular to say, Magnus got up and went on again, leaving poor Joe not only still in the rear, but without time even for a rest.

All this astonishing activity, as I said, was the result, not of energy, but of bad temper. The worse their tempers became the greater the pace, and the greater the pace the nearer the top of that interminable ridge. Towards the end it was uncommonly like running. Magnus would have given worlds to venture to look behind and see how the idiot below was fagging; and Joe would have given a lot to see the lout above come a cropper and smash his leg. It wants a pretty hot friendship to stand the test of a mountain-side.

At last (without a suspicion of what o'clock it was, or how far they had come), Magnus actually stopped and lay down.

"Serves him right," said Joe, triumphantly, running with all his might to take advantage of his chance. Alas! when he got up to his friend, he discovered that after all he was not dead-beat, or wounded, or ill.

The reason he had stopped was that he had got to the top.

As was natural, as soon as this agreeable and amazing discovery was made, Magnus minor and my brother Joe forgot their rancour and loved one another again with a mighty affection. Their own brothers weren't in it.

"Good old Joey!" cried Magnus, as my brother lay on the turf beside him; "crowd in, old hoss—lots of room!"

"Good old Magny!" responded Joe; "what a day we're having!"

Presently they condescended to look about them. They were on a sharp ridge, one side of which sloped down into the valley from which they had ascended, the other looked out on an uninterrupted prospect of cloud and mist.

"This isn't what's-his-name at all," said Joe. "There's a tuck shop on the top of it—there's none here."

"That chap was right," said Magnus. "That must be Snowdon over there—we've missed him."

"Horrid bore," said Joe, who, however, regretted the mountain less than the tuck shop.

The afternoon was changing. The clouds were beginning to sweep up from the other side and begriming the sky which had been so ruthlessly clear all the morning.

All of a sudden the mist below them parted, and disclosed through a frame of cloud a great cauldron of rock yawning at their feet, at the bottom of which—as it seemed, miles below—lay a black lake. It was a scene Dante could have described better than I.

"If we could get down there we could have a tub," said Magnus.

"It's snug enough up here," replied the poet; "don't you think so?" Magnus admitted it was snug, and did not press his motion. For, though he scorned to say so, he was fagged, and felt he could do with a half- hour's lounge before undertaking a new venture.

So the reconciled friends took their siesta on the top of the mysterious mountain, and, in doing so, oddly enough fell asleep.

SUB-CHAPTER II

THE IMMORTALS

When they woke, the sun was still shining; but it had got round to the side of them which, when they dropped off, had been wrapped in cloud, while the mist had taken possession of the valley and hillside by which they had ascended.

The transformation scene was so complete that had they not seen Joe's paper on the ground beside them, and recognised the bank of heather against which they reclined, they would have found it difficult to say exactly where they were.

To all appearances they were at the end of the world. The great cauldron gaped below them, apparently perpendicular on every side, enclosing in its depths the black lake, on whose still surface the rays of the sun gleamed weirdly and gloomily.

Not a sound was to be heard except a distant sullen rumble, which might have been thunder, or earthquake, or the six-o'clock train going back to Llandudno. Above them, as the clouds drifted past, they could see, as they lay on their backs, occasional glimpses of blue, and sometimes in the far distance a shining peak bathed in crimson light.

All this was natural enough; and, were it not that they had their return tickets in their pockets, Magnus minor and Joe would probably have been content to enjoy the show for an hour or so.

What did concern them, when they got to their feet, was to observe that, so far from being as they supposed, and could have testified on solemn affidavit, on the top of the mountain, the ground now appeared to rise on every side except that occupied by the cauldron.

Whichever way they tried to walk they found themselves going uphill.

"Rum start," said Magnus minor, after ramping round in a semicircle and finding no trace of their homeward path. "It strikes me we shall have to hang out here till the clouds roll by, Joey."

"All very well. How about grub?" said the poet. "We shall be just about what-do-you-call-it by then."

"Hullo," said Magnus, looking at his watch, "do you know it's 11 p.m. and broad daylight."

Joe consulted his watch, and wound it up as he did so.

"So it is—must be a thingamybob—a roaring boreali, or whatever you call it, going on. Wouldn't be so bad if it was good to eat."

Magnus assented, and the two outcasts stood and watched with somewhat mingled feelings the battalion of clouds as they swirled past and soared up at the heights above.

"May as well go upstairs too," said the poet, dismally. So they began the ascent. This time Magnus showed no inclination to forge ahead, and Joe took every precaution not to lag behind. In fact, they proceeded arm in arm, trying to enjoy it, but inwardly wondering who would have the benefit of their supper at Llandudno.

It was easy enough going; the turf was crisp and soft, and as they got up a little, flowers began to peep out. Though they could not see through the mists, they fancied they could catch the sound of birds and the splash of water. The clouds, sweeping up on every side, seemed to help them along, so that sometimes they could hardly be quite sure whether they were walking on earth or air. Altogether, had they but dined, they would have voted the walk one of the jolliest they ever had in their lives.

Presently a strange sound above brought them suddenly to a halt. It was music of some sort, but mingling with it the even sweeter music of plates and knives and forks; and when for a moment the music ceased, they seemed to detect voices and laughter.

"Some fellows having a picnic," said Magnus, joyfully; "keep it up, chappie, and we shall get some of the pickings— you see."

"Give them a—what-do-you-call-it?" said Joe. Whereupon Magnus startled the air with a loud "coo-oo-ey!"

The sounds above ceased all of a sudden, and the weather seemed to change to thundery.

Then a faint echo of the shout came back, and almost immediately afterwards a gentleman appeared through the mist.

He was a young-looking man, who had apparently been bathing, and had not had time to dress after it. He wore a curious sort of cap, with a wing sticking out at either side, and carried in his hand a very elaborately carved walking-stick.

"Please, can you tell us the way down to Llanberis?" asked Magnus, thinking it better not to appear to notice the gentleman's *deshabille*.

The gentleman stared at the two boys in a startled sort of way, and shrugged his shoulders.

"A foreigner," said Joe. "Try him in—what's-its—name—French."

"*S'il vous plait, pouvez vous dire nous le chemin a bas a Llanberis*?" said Magnus, who was a capital French scholar.

It was not at all certain that the gentleman understood even this. He pointed with his thumb over his shoulder up at the clouds, which was certainly not the shortest way down to Llanberis. But as it was the direction from which the sound of the knives and forks had proceeded, it seemed as if nothing would be lost by following.

The gentleman, who in his excitement had clean forgotten about his garments, hurried the boys up the hill at a terrific pace, until all of a sudden they got out of the clouds and saw clear ahead.

The scene was a remarkable one—Magnus's idea of a picnic had been a correct, one. But such a picnic!

A party of some fifteen persons, not by any means all gentlemen, was sitting round a medium-sized table, spread with cups and dishes. The entire company, if they had not been bathing, were apparently preparing to do so, except one gentleman, who was so encased in armour that it would have been a very tedious job to take it off, and one lady, who was also got up in a military fashion, and carried a very ugly shield on her arm. The person at the head of the table was an imposing-looking gentleman, who held a sort of stuffed football in his hand, and had a tame eagle perched on his shoulder. Near him was a very good-looking, self-satisfied fellow with long curls, who had evidently been entertaining the company with a performance on a Jew's harp. Then there was a lame old gentleman, who looked as if he would be all the better for his bath when the time came, who carried a big sledge-hammer in his hand; and another fishy sort of person, who flourished about with a three-pronged pitchfork. A very cross-looking lady sat next to the gentleman at the head of the table. By the way she kept her eye upon him, contradicting every word he said, and snubbing him at every opportunity, she was evidently his wife. Another good-looking lady was playing with a very pert-looking boy, who wore a pair of toy wings on his shoulders, and appeared to be a general favourite with every one except the other ladies, who seemed generally a disagreeable lot, and not at all good form in their manners at table.

The refreshments were being served by a nice-looking housemaid and a page-boy, who had their work cut out for them in keeping every one supplied. For these ladies and gentlemen, whatever else may be said of them, had uncommonly good appetites.

Magnus minor and Joe were too busy at first taking stock of the provender to devote much attention to the picnic party itself; but when at last they did take a look round, each uttered a cry of consternation, and crowded up to his chum for protection.

"Joey," said Magnus, "don't you know them?"

"Rather," said Joe. "I could tell them at once from the likenesses in—what do you call him's—Smith's classical thingamybob. It's Olympus, after all!"

"So it is," groaned Magnus. "Oh, Jupiter!"

At the mention of his name, the gentleman at the head of the table looked up.

"I beg your pardon," said he, in fairly good English.

His manner rather overawed the two boys, who thought it wise to be civil to begin with, at any rate.

So they touched their caps, and Magnus said—

"Do you happen to know the shortest cut down to Llanberis, sir?"

"We've lost our way, don't you know," said Joe; "and we've got to catch the last train back to—you know—what's-his-name—Llandudno."

Jove looked a little scared, and, by way of intimating that he did not understand a word, shook his head.

"I wish you wouldn't shake your head," said Juno, the lady next to him; "it upsets everything, and makes the glasses spill. Why can't you say, like a man, you don't understand German? Who are your friends, pray? We've quite enough boys about the place without any more. What is it, you boys? We've nothing for you!"

"Poor boys," said the good-looking lady before mentioned; "they look quite hungry."

"So we are," said Magnus. "*Ainsi nous sommes.*"

"*Tout droit*" said Venus (that was her name), with a smile across the table at the gentleman with the Jew's harp; "*vous aurez quelque chose a manger dans une seconde.* Make room for the boys, Vulcan. We'll excuse you."

Here the lame gentleman with the murky face slowly hobbled up, apparently greatly relieved to be allowed to go. And Magnus minor and Joe, without further invitation, crowded in at the table between Venus and the lady with the shield.

"Beasts, all of them," whispered Magnus to his friend, "and it don't look much of a spread; but it's better than nothing. Here, Tommy," said he, addressing the page-boy, "*quelque de cela*—do you hear?"

Tommy (whose real name was Ganymede), obeyed with alacrity, and put before each a plate of what looked like very flowery mashed potato, and a small glass of a frothy beverage.

"I suppose this is what they call nectar and ambrosia," said Magnus. "I'd like to catch them giving us such stuff at school."

"Plenty of it, that's one thing," said Joe. "I fancy we can keep young what's-his-name going for half an hour or so comfortably."

"Well, my dear, and how do you like Olympus?" said the lady with the shield.

"Oh, I dare say *you're* all right," said Joe, diplomatically; "but I don't think much of the rest."

"What did he say?" inquired Juno from the end of the table.

"Never mind," said Minerva, "we're having a little friendly chat; you need not interfere."

"You're talking about me, I know you are," said Juno.

Talbot Baines Reed

"*Non, nous ne sommes pas*," said Joe.

"Never mind her," said Minerva; "she doesn't count for much here. Of course, you know the gentleman opposite with the lyre—my brother, Apollo, the poet."

"Is he? I say," cried Joe, across the table, "Mr Apollo, do you know anything that rhymes with 'catsup'?"

Apollo smiled rather foolishly, and said he fancied it was not in the rhyming dictionary; at least, he never had to use the word in his day.

Joe's opinion of a poet who could not rhyme any word in the language fell considerably.

"He means well, does Polly," said Minerva, apologetically; "but he never had a public-school education, you know."

Magnus meanwhile was making himself agreeable to his fair neighbour.

"I say," said he, in the midst of his fourth helping of ambrosia, "which is the fellow who once kicked the other fellow downstairs?"

Venus laughed immoderately.

"The other fellow is my husband, the poor dear who made room for you just now. The fellow that kicked him down is Jupiter—there!"

"Good old Jupiter!" said Magnus. "I'd like to see you do it again. Did you do it with a place-kick, or a drop, or a punt?"

"It's no use speaking to my husband," said Juno, "he can't

hear; and if he could, he's too ignorant to understand. He's getting old."

"You must be getting on yourself," said Magnus. "I remember hearing my grandfather say he knew you very well when he was a boy."

Juno bridled up angrily at this, which was the signal for a round of laughter from every one else, and a scene might have ensued had not Apollo at the moment struck up his lyre and drowned everybody's voice. He wasn't a particularly good player, and his instrument was of a cheap make. But the noise served to keep the peace, which was all that was ever wanted.

Presently the meal ended, and the two boys were very glad to get up and stretch their legs. After the heavy supper they had had, they felt bound to be moderately civil; and some of the ladies and gentlemen—especially the former—made themselves agreeable enough. But they could not get on at all with some of the men. Mars, the fellow in armour, was one of these. He was a horribly conceited snob, they agreed, and only wore his armour because it was a new suit, and he thought he looked well in it.

"Well, my little men," said he, grandly, as they came up, "so you have come to see the great god of war? I will not hurt you. Try to lift my spear. It weighs two hundredweight and some odd pounds. You have heard, no doubt, of some of my achievements?"

"Oh yes," said Magnus minor; "you were the chap that got a hiding outside Troy from Diomed, and yelled enough to bring the roof down."

"Ha, ha! Good old Diomed!" said Joe.

Mars turned red and white with anger, and said that if it were not too much trouble he would like to knock their two impudent heads together, at which they and every one else laughed all the more.

"You boys," said Venus, coming up opportunely at this point, "here is a friend I know you will like to meet. He's just the sort of person boys admire. He's not one of our regular party, you know; but we ask him in to dessert now and then—don't we, Hercules?"

"How do you do?" said Magnus, holding out his hand to a great stout gentleman, who wore a rug over his shoulders and carried a club in his hand. "Done all your jobs—swabbed out those stables yet?"

The stout gentleman flushed up a little at this allusion, and said something in Greek which fortunately the boys did not understand.

"Been having any more lessons on the sewing machine lately—eh, old chap?" inquired Joe. "We know all about you, Magnus minor and I. There's fellows at our school could lick you into a cocked hat. You come to our sports one day and see."

Hercules, a good deal ruffled, used a considerable amount of idiomatic Greek, and made for the boys with his club.

Fortunately for them, Minerva's shield happened to be lying on the ground close by, and Joe, with great presence of mind, recalling his classics for the occasion, took it up and presented it at the giant.

Naturally, he turned to stone on the spot; and as at that particular moment he had one foot off the ground, his club above his head, and his mouth wide open, the effect was striking.

They amused themselves for a short time playing Aunt Sally at him; and then, getting rather tired of the whole affair, looked about them for some way of escaping.

They met Cupid, the boy that belonged to Venus, prowling about with his bow and arrow.

"Hullo, kid!" said Magnus. "Here you are—three shots a penny, and twopence if you hit me at twenty yards!"

Cupid aimed and missed, and then very foolishly began to cry.

"What are you blubbering at?" asked Joe. "You young soft!"

Cupid said he was miserable. Everybody up there bullied him, and he couldn't hit anything nowadays with his bow and arrows.

"Jack it up then, and come to our school," said Magnus, slapping him on the back. "Lots of larks there. You can wear Etons and a topper, and chum in our study—can't he, Joe?"

"Yes, if he likes to do his share of the fagging," said Joe.

"I don't much mind what I do, as long as I get away from this lot."

"All serene; come down with us. We're hanging out at Llandudno for the holidays. My mater will take you in, I'm certain."

"Ah, yes, and by the way," said Joe, once more making a

Talbot Baines Reed

brilliant dive into his classics, "there's a friend of yours, you know, called what's- her-name, only a few doors off. Isn't there, Magnus?"

"Rather!" said Magnus, who had not a notion what was being referred to.

"You don't mean to say Psyche—"

"That's her—the very article; rather a wonner, too. Magnus is spoons on her, you know," added Joe, with a wink at his friend; "but he'll back out for you."

"Oh," said Magnus, blushing, "it don't matter to me. Besides, she's going to-morrow."

This settled matters.

"Let's cut," said Cupid, impatiently, "or we shall be too late."

A great row was going on among the gods. Goodness knows what it was about—nobody ever did know that! Venus and Juno were scratching one another's faces; Jupiter was shaking his fist and thundering all round; the other men were arguing in high Greek, and the other ladies were screaming at the top of their voices.

"They're at it again," said Cupid, making a wry face. "That sort of thing goes on here from morning to night. We shan't be missed. Come on, you fellows!"

Down they went at a great pace, Cupid (who was much less encumbered with clothes than the other two) showing a lead. Presently they lost sight of the top, and through the clouds below caught a distant glimpse of the black lake.

"Can't we take a short cut down there?" asked Joe.

"Not good enough," said Cupid. "That's where Charon hangs out; and he and I don't hit it off. No, we'd better go down to where you went asleep, and then trot down by the track to Llanberis. I know the way—come on."

They followed, wondering at the pace at which they went. In scarce five minutes from the top they stood on the spot where they had first halted hours and hours ago.

There a remarkable thing happened.

Cupid, who had all along seemed the most eager of the three to escape into the valley, suddenly halted, spread his little wings, and with a merry laugh began to fly upwards.

"Hold on," said Magnus; "that's not the way down, you young cad!"

"Ha, ha!" said Cupid, rising higher. In vain they besought him to stay. He only laughed, and soared higher and higher and—

* * * * *

The next thing they were aware of was that they were lying on their backs, waking up from their sleep, and watching a white gull skimming the air overhead, and crying out seaward.

Whether they had been to Olympus at all, or had only dreamt it, they could never say. The one thing they did know was that they just managed to catch the last train that night back to Llandudno, where they found supper waiting them.

Choose from Thousands of 1stWorldLibrary Classics By

A. M. Barnard
Ada Leverson
Adolphus William Ward
Aesop
Agatha Christie
Alexander Aaronsohn
Alexander Kielland
Alexandre Dumas
Alfred Gatty
Alfred Ollivant
Alice Duer Miller
Alice Turner Curtis
Alice Dunbar
Allen Chapman
Alleyne Ireland
Ambrose Bierce
Amelia E. Barr
Amory H. Bradford
Andrew Lang
Andrew McFarland Davis
Andy Adams
Angela Brazil
Anna Alice Chapin
Anna Sewell
Annie Besant
Annie Hamilton Donnell
Annie Payson Call
Annie Roe Carr
Annonaymous
Anton Chekhov
Archibald Lee Fletcher
Arnold Bennett
Arthur C. Benson
Arthur Conan Doyle
Arthur M. Winfield
Arthur Ransome
Arthur Schnitzler
Arthur Train
Atticus
B.H. Baden-Powell
B. M. Bower
B. C. Chatterjee
Baroness Emmuska Orczy
Baroness Orczy
Basil King
Bayard Taylor
Ben Macomber
Bertha Muzzy Bower
Bjornstjerne Bjornson

Booth Tarkington
Boyd Cable
Bram Stoker
C. Collodi
C. E. Orr
C. M. Ingleby
Carolyn Wells
Catherine Parr Traill
Charles A. Eastman
Charles Amory Beach
Charles Dickens
Charles Dudley Warner
Charles Farrar Browne
Charles Ives
Charles Kingsley
Charles Klein
Charles Hanson Towne
Charles Lathrop Pack
Charles Romyn Dake
Charles Whibley
Charles Willing Beale
Charlotte M. Braeme
Charlotte M. Yonge
Charlotte Perkins Stetson
Clair W. Hayes
Clarence Day Jr.
Clarence E. Mulford
Clemence Housman
Confucius
Coningsby Dawson
Cornelis DeWitt Wilcox
Cyril Burleigh
D. H. Lawrence
Daniel Defoe
David Garnett
Dinah Craik
Don Carlos Janes
Donald Keyhoe
Dorothy Kilner
Dougan Clark
Douglas Fairbanks
E. Nesbit
E. P. Roe
E. Phillips Oppenheim
E. S. Brooks
Earl Barnes
Edgar Rice Burroughs
Edith Van Dyne
Edith Wharton

Edward Everett Hale
Edward J. O'Biren
Edward S. Ellis
Edwin L. Arnold
Eleanor Atkins
Eleanor Hallowell Abbott
Eliot Gregory
Elizabeth Gaskell
Elizabeth McCracken
Elizabeth Von Arnim
Ellem Key
Emerson Hough
Emilie F. Carlen
Emily Bronte
Emily Dickinson
Enid Bagnold
Enilor Macartney Lane
Erasmus W. Jones
Ernie Howard Pie
Ethel May Dell
Ethel Turner
Ethel Watts Mumford
Eugene Sue
Eugenie Foa
Eugene Wood
Eustace Hale Ball
Evelyn Everett-green
Everard Cotes
F. H. Cheley
F. J. Cross
F. Marion Crawford
Fannie E. Newberry
Federick Austin Ogg
Ferdinand Ossendowski
Fergus Hume
Florence A. Kilpatrick
Fremont B. Deering
Francis Bacon
Francis Darwin
Frances Hodgson Burnett
Frances Parkinson Keyes
Frank Gee Patchin
Frank Harris
Frank Jewett Mather
Frank L. Packard
Frank V. Webster
Frederic Stewart Isham
Frederick Trevor Hill
Frederick Winslow Taylor

Friedrich Kerst
Friedrich Nietzsche
Fyodor Dostoyevsky
G.A. Henty
G.K. Chesterton
Gabrielle E. Jackson
Garrett P. Serviss
Gaston Leroux
George A. Warren
George Ade
Geroge Bernard Shaw
George Cary Eggleston
George Durston
George Ebers
George Eliot
George Gissing
George MacDonald
George Meredith
George Orwell
George Sylvester Viereck
George Tucker
George W. Cable
George Wharton James
Gertrude Atherton
Gordon Casserly
Grace E. King
Grace Gallatin
Grace Greenwood
Grant Allen
Guillermo A. Sherwell
Gulielma Zollinger
Gustav Flaubert
H. A. Cody
H. B. Irving
H. C. Bailey
H. G. Wells
H. H. Munro
H. Irving Hancock
H. R. Naylor
H. Rider Haggard
H. W. C. Davis
Haldeman Julius
Hall Caine
Hamilton Wright Mabie
Hans Christian Andersen
Harold Avery
Harold McGrath
Harriet Beecher Stowe
Harry Castlemon
Harry Coghill
Harry Houidini

Hayden Carruth
Helent Hunt Jackson
Helen Nicolay
Hendrik Conscience
Hendy David Thoreau
Henri Barbusse
Henrik Ibsen
Henry Adams
Henry Ford
Henry Frost
Henry James
Henry Jones Ford
Henry Seton Merriman
Henry W Longfellow
Herbert A. Giles
Herbert Carter
Herbert N. Casson
Herman Hesse
Hildegard G. Frey
Homer
Honore De Balzac
Horace B. Day
Horace Walpole
Horatio Alger Jr.
Howard Pyle
Howard R. Garis
Hugh Lofting
Hugh Walpole
Humphry Ward
Ian Maclaren
Inez Haynes Gillmore
Irving Bacheller
Isabel Cecilia Williams
Isabel Hornibrook
Israel Abrahams
Ivan Turgenev
J. G.Austin
J. Henri Fabre
J. M. Barrie
J. M. Walsh
J. Macdonald Oxley
J. R. Miller
J. S. Fletcher
J. S. Knowles
J. Storer Clouston
J. W. Duffield
Jack London
Jacob Abbott
James Allen
James Andrews
James Baldwin

James Branch Cabell
James DeMille
James Joyce
James Lane Allen
James Lane Allen
James Oliver Curwood
James Oppenheim
James Otis
James R. Driscoll
Jane Abbott
Jane Austen
Jane L. Stewart
Janet Aldridge
Jens Peter Jacobsen
Jerome K. Jerome
Jessie Graham Flower
John Buchan
John Burroughs
John Cournos
John F. Kennedy
John Gay
John Glasworthy
John Habberton
John Joy Bell
John Kendrick Bangs
John Milton
John Philip Sousa
John Taintor Foote
Jonas Lauritz Idemil Lie
Jonathan Swift
Joseph A. Altsheler
Joseph Carey
Joseph Conrad
Joseph E. Badger Jr
Joseph Hergesheimer
Joseph Jacobs
Jules Vernes
Julian Hawthrone
Julie A Lippmann
Justin Huntly McCarthy
Kakuzo Okakura
Karle Wilson Baker
Kate Chopin
Kenneth Grahame
Kenneth McGaffey
Kate Langley Bosher
Kate Langley Bosher
Katherine Cecil Thurston
Katherine Stokes
L. A. Abbot
L. T. Meade

L. Frank Baum	Paul G. Tomlinson	T. S. Arthur
Latta Griswold	Paul Severing	The Princess Der Ling
Laura Dent Crane	Percy Brebner	Thomas A. Janvier
Laura Lee Hope	Percy Keese Fitzhugh	Thomas A Kempis
Laurence Housman	Peter B. Kyne	Thomas Anderton
Lawrence Beasley	Plato	Thomas Bailey Aldrich
Leo Tolstoy	Quincy Allen	Thomas Bulfinch
Leonid Andreyev	R. Derby Holmes	Thomas De Quincey
Lewis Carroll	R. L. Stevenson	Thomas Dixon
Lewis Sperry Chafer	R. S. Ball	Thomas H. Huxley
Lilian Bell	Rabindranath Tagore	Thomas Hardy
Lloyd Osbourne	Rahul Alvares	Thomas More
Louis Hughes	Ralph Bonehill	Thornton W. Burgess
Louis Joseph Vance	Ralph Henry Barbour	U. S. Grant
Louis Tracy	Ralph Victor	Upton Sinclair
Louisa May Alcott	Ralph Waldo Emmerson	Valentine Williams
Lucy Fitch Perkins	Rene Descartes	Various Authors
Lucy Maud Montgomery	Ray Cummings	Vaughan Kester
Luther Benson	Rex Beach	Victor Appleton
Lydia Miller Middleton	Rex E. Beach	Victor G. Durham
Lyndon Orr	Richard Harding Davis	Victoria Cross
M. Corvus	Richard Jefferies	Virginia Woolf
M. H. Adams	Richard Le Gallienne	Wadsworth Camp
Margaret E. Sangster	Robert Barr	Walter Camp
Margret Howth	Robert Frost	Walter Scott
Margaret Vandercook	Robert Gordon Anderson	Washington Irving
Margaret W. Hungerford	Robert L. Drake	Wilbur Lawton
Margret Penrose	Robert Lansing	Wilkie Collins
Maria Edgeworth	Robert Lynd	Willa Cather
Maria Thompson Daviess	Robert Michael Ballantyne	Willard F. Baker
Mariano Azuela	Robert W. Chambers	William Dean Howells
Marion Polk Angellotti	Rosa Nouchette Carey	William le Queux
Mark Overton	Rudyard Kipling	W. Makepeace Thackeray
Mark Twain	Saint Augustine	William W. Walter
Mary Austin	Samuel B. Allison	William Shakespeare
Mary Catherine Crowley	Samuel Hopkins Adams	Winston Churchill
Mary Cole	Sarah Bernhardt	Yei Theodora Ozaki
Mary Hastings Bradley	Sarah C. Hallowell	Yogi Ramacharaka
Mary Roberts Rinehart	Selma Lagerlof	Young E. Allison
Mary Rowlandson	Sherwood Anderson	Zane Grey
M. Wollstonecraft Shelley	Sigmund Freud	
Maud Lindsay	Standish O'Grady	
Max Beerbohm	Stanley Weyman	
Myra Kelly	Stella Benson	
Nathaniel Hawthrone	Stella M. Francis	
Nicolo Machiavelli	Stephen Crane	
O. F. Walton	Stewart Edward White	
Oscar Wilde	Stijn Streuvels	
Owen Johnson	Swami Abhedananda	
P.G. Wodehouse	Swami Parmananda	
Paul and Mabel Thorne	T. S. Ackland	

www.ingramcontent.com/pod-product-compliance
Lightning Source LLC
Chambersburg PA
CBHW020436270626
47155CB00022B/492